Outdoor Navigation

Handbook for Tutors

by Pat & Brian Mee

on behalf of the

National Navigation Award Scheme

a step in the right direction

HARVEY

Published and distributed by:

HARVEY, 12 - 22 Main Street, Doune, Perthshire FK16 6BJ
Tel: 01786 841202   Fax: 01786 841098
email: sales@harveymaps.co.uk

First edition   2010
Reprinted   2014

ISBN 978-185137002-3

Acknowledgements
Members of the NNAS Board for constructive advice on the content and layout. In particular, Sue Harvey, Keith Rugg, Anne Salisbury and Julian Tippett.
Julian Tippett for providing the basis for the 'Walk Planning' and 'Sources of Further Information' sections.
Derek Sheehan for proof reading the content.
Derek Allison, Steve Long and Nigel Williams for reviewing the content.
HARVEY for software and production support.

National Navigation Award Scheme
33 Stirling Enterprise Park,
Springbank Road,
Stirling FK7 7RP
Tel: 01786 451307
Fax: 01786 445703
Email: info@nnas.org.uk
www.nnas.org.uk

 NNAS
a step in the right direction

 British Orienteering    Royal Institute of Navigation
Science Technology Practice

 SUUNTO   MOUNTAIN TRAINING

The Authors

Pat Mee

Pat is a specialist PE teacher who made a career move into outdoor education. For 15 years, she was Head of an LEA inner city outdoor centre. She is now a freelance tutor.

She has worked on many ML and WGL (now known as H&ML) courses. She runs British Orienteering Coach courses for local authorities along with staff training courses in outdoor & adventurous activities. For 10 years, she was a professional Development Officer for a local orienteering organisation.

Pat is Lead Officer for the Certificate in Basic Expedition Leadership and has key links with the major outdoor organisations such as MLT and OEAP. She also works in the qualifications industry and has played a leading role in awards development. This includes the 1st4Sport Certificates in Coaching Orienteering, endorsed by UKCC on behalf of British Orienteering.

Brian Mee

Brian originally worked in mechanical engineering with a spell as a technical writer before moving into education as a teacher of mathematics. He has long been an enthusiast in a wide range of outdoor activities and has worked part time as an instructor or coach in many of them.

He now provides technical support to Pat's freelance work including mapping of local parks and school grounds. As a self-taught amateur he goes to considerable lengths to produce high quality artwork for training materials.

His technical background, broad outdoor experience, knowledge of teaching and familiarity with modern coaching practices have allowed him to contribute hugely to the content of this book. His ability to simultaneously produce the artwork has been highly beneficial.

Contents

Foreword

Knowing how to find your way around in the world, whether locally, nationally or internationally is a particularly useful life skill.

Confident route finding is the key that unlocks the enjoyment of travelling to and through places in the countryside.

There can be no doubt about the huge benefits of exercising in the outdoors. To be able to do so responsibly, understanding rights of way and being responsible stewards of the countryside are some of the aims of the National Navigation Award Scheme. Another is providing people with authoritative training to enable full enjoyment of their outings.

Sadly we sometimes hear about people equipped with map and compass who lose their way and need to be guided from the hills by the mountain rescue teams. Similarly there are those who fear to step from tried and tested paths or tracks lest they trespass or get lost.

Beginners to navigation, as well as the more experienced, can undertake National Navigation Award Scheme courses to further their knowledge and understanding of both the science and especially the art of navigation.

The scheme also addresses the wish for accreditation by some youth groups. It is complementary to the Duke of Edinburgh's Award expedition navigation, scouts and guides awards schemes, military cadet groups, Walking Your Way to Health groups and many more.

Young people especially, have a yearning for challenge and adventure and this can be achieved by heading off into the countryside by themselves. Help and guidance rather than restrictions are the key to a successful experience. Working with the progressive NNAS scheme allows people to experience the excitement and the associated sense of achievement brought about by journeys to new places.

This book has taken a considerable time to produce but the wait was worthwhile. It is aimed at those who teach, train or coach others in navigation and discusses progression and techniques rather than focusing on individual skills which are amply described in many existing publications.

The material has been drawn from a number of sources, including NNAS workshops and personal contributions from NNAS Directors and providers, but the content you see here has been designed and written by Pat and Brian Mee. All contributors have many years of experience of teaching and assessing navigation at the highest levels. Production of this book has been a voluntary labour of love by Pat and Brian. The Directors are indebted to them for their tenacity, diligence and creativity in ensuring that the book is of the highest quality.

I know that trainers new and old will find something useful in this book.

Thank you to all who take the time to make the teaching of navigation practical, fun and rewarding for their candidates.

Without doubt, "a step in the right direction".

Anne Salisbury

NNAS Chair
Senior Inspector - Adventure Activities Licensing Service

March 2010

Photo: Dave Gittus

Peter Palmer

Peter Palmer, a great visionary and philosopher, founded the National Navigation Award Scheme in 1994. He was the Scheme's only chair and development leader until he passed away in 2003 after a long illness.

Peter had two abiding interests in life; teaching and orienteering. Through his work as a secondary school teacher and his high level involvement in coaching orienteering, along with a considerable knowledge of navigation skills and techniques, he successfully amassed the expertise to launch and develop the Scheme. Peter also produced a small tutor handbook which served as a useful planning resource up to now.

An important aim in creating the Scheme was to encourage independent exploration and enjoyment of the countryside by children and people of all ages through the self-confidence that arises from navigational competence. Thousands of people have since benefitted from these principles through NNAS courses.

We are confident that Peter would wholeheartedly endorse the developments that have followed on from his foundation work. This new book serves as a fitting tribute to the enthusiasm and inspiration that Peter provided.

Preface

This book is the first large-scale attempt to explore the issues involved in tutoring navigation for walkers. The National Navigation Award Scheme has taken on board this project to provide a valuable resource for course planning and delivery.

The content of the book is structured with a view to tutors who deliver the NNAS Navigator Awards but it should be of value to any navigation instructor.

The book outlines the principles for good tutoring. It has separate sections for the Bronze, Silver and Gold Navigator Awards that provide ideas and sample training exercises. An outline of modern assessment practice is included as good assessment forms an important part of any course. Finally, a list of relevant information sources is provided.

A major principle of this book is seeking to avoid indoor theory sessions wherever this is practicable. With good research and planning, the majority of navigation topics can be tutored outdoors. Navigation is, after all, a practical subject that lends itself to such an approach. While bad weather will sometimes enforce indoor sessions, they too can be made enjoyable with the right approach.

Imagine the benefits of outdoor-based courses for students: they will learn in a realistic environment that should immediately provide interesting and motivational experiences. With good planning, most learning exercises can involve all students for most of the time to maintain their enthusiasm. With the right approach, learning navigation can be fun.

It goes without saying that courses of this nature do not happen by accident. They require a considerable time commitment to plan precisely what to teach, find good tutoring areas and avoid overloading the student at any one time. Courses ideally need to be structured so that a new topic follows on naturally from previous learning. Such an approach can only succeed with a high level of enthusiasm from the tutor. The reward though, is greater satisfaction for both student and tutor. A well-run course also serves as a valuable delivery model for students who may later decide to become tutors themselves.

This book is designed to assist the full range of tutors from those who are just beginning to those with many years of experience. The main focus of the handbook is on principles and ideas for tutoring. It assumes that tutors will generally be familiar with the main skills and techniques of navigation through personal experience and through existing literature.

Not all navigation skills and techniques are covered in all books on navigation. Neither do all books cover them in adequate depth from a tutoring point of view. Discussion of some skills and techniques is therefore included in this handbook where it is felt that tutors may benefit from the points made.

The book is not prescriptive; rather it seeks to serve as a stimulus to imaginative tutoring. There are many approaches to tutoring navigation and only the tutor can decide on the best approach to use for specific individuals. Neither is the book exhaustive; rather it seeks to augment the literature that is already available. Tutors are urged to study the large amount of information on navigation that can be found in many books and magazine articles to assist with the planning and delivery process.

British Orienteering offers many valuable ideas for tutoring navigation via the content of its coaching awards and supporting literature. Whilst some ideas may need adapting to suit walkers, they provide a useful foundation especially for the inexperienced tutor. There are also several books available on coaching orienteering.

A further avenue for developing course delivery methods exists through working alongside other tutors with a view to exchanging ideas. Every year, NNAS offers tutor workshops in different parts of the country to provide opportunities for discussion.

NNAS urges all tutors of navigation to devote the time needed to plan exciting courses. NNAS hopes that the production of this book will provide the impetus.

The National Navigation Award Scheme

The Structure of the Scheme

The National Navigation Award Scheme is administered by a Board of highly experienced navigators and outdoor industry representatives. Courses are delivered and assessed by registered providers with appropriate leader qualifications throughout the UK. The Scheme offers two sets of navigation awards.

Outdoor Discovery Awards

The Outdoor Discovery Awards encourage the exploration of local areas using simple maps such as street maps, pictorial and park maps, and orienteering maps. There is a gradual learning progression via One Star, Two Star and Three Star levels. The awards are aimed at all age groups and are also beneficial for people who need to learn at a slower pace.

Navigator Awards

The Navigator Awards cover the full range of skills for competent navigation in all terrain types in any area of the UK. They are offered at Bronze Navigator, Silver Navigator and Gold Navigator levels.

Assessment is aimed primarily at navigation skills. All courses, however, include issues such as weather, access and conservation, safety, walking skills, etc.

Award Overlaps

The Three Star Outdoor Discovery Award and the Bronze Navigator Award overlap slightly in that both cover the beginnings of handrail navigation.

Tutor Resources

Each award system has separate tutor resources. This particular book is specifically designed to support delivery of the Navigator Awards. It may, however, offer limited information for tutors who deliver the Three Star Outdoor Discovery Award.

NNAS & Other Award Scheme Titles

The nomenclature adopted by NNAS for its Award titles is entirely for its own specific purposes. Direct comparison with similar terminology in other schemes is not necessarily appropriate. The Bronze Navigator Award skills, for example, may well suffice for Silver Expeditions in the Duke of Edinburgh's Award depending on the expedition location.

About the Navigator Awards

The Navigator Awards primarily meet the needs of walkers but they could be of value to participants in any activity involving navigation. However, tutors should not depart radically from the syllabus to accommodate other activity interests.

Where can an Award Holder Walk?

On gaining a Navigator Award, candidates should be advised that their choice of walking area and ability to walk safely is entirely their own responsibility. Decisions on where to walk should take account of the skills they have learned along with previous experience, weather conditions, fitness, access rights and responsibilities, etc. The tutor can generalise on the issues involved in making route choices but making specific route recommendations may have legal implications in the event of an accident.

The Remit for Course Delivery

It is preferable to deliver and assess courses in terrain that facilitates considerable navigation practice within a relatively small area. The terrain descriptions below indicate typical areas to be used at each level:

Bronze Navigator Award

Gentle, rolling terrain in lowland areas with well-defined boundary features where navigation will be primarily on roads, tracks and well defined paths.

Routes should also include other line features such as walls and forest boundaries. The compass will be used only to set the map and check route direction using the orientated map. Route finding accuracy will be checked against adjacent point features, walls, fences, forest boundaries and major relief features. Typical areas at the upper limit for courses are the White Peak, Chiltern Hills, Clwyd Hills and Pentland Hills (eastern end).

Silver Navigator Award

Relatively small areas of open country with well-defined boundary features.

Navigation will require use of the Bronze skills along with additional line features such as streams, indistinct paths, etc. It should also include routes in moderate hill country that avoid steep slopes and mountainous terrain. Short crossings of open country will be made using compass bearings with the emphasis on learning techniques rather than excessive distance. Route finding accuracy will be checked against smaller contour features than at Bronze e.g. small valleys, minor hills, etc. Typical areas at the upper limit for courses are the Yorkshire Dales, Shropshire Hills, Brecon Beacons and Ochil Hills.

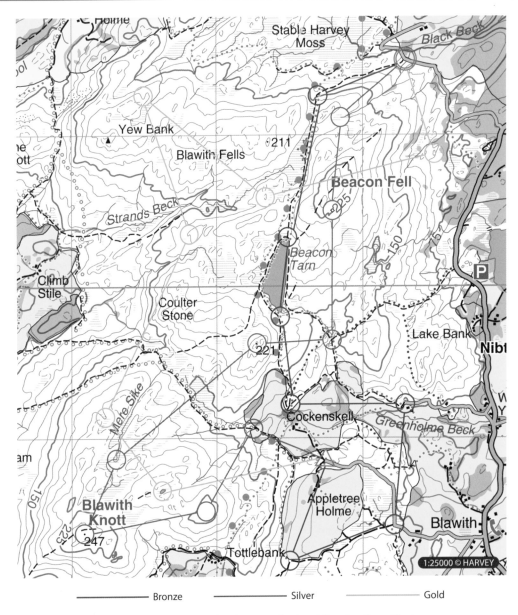

———————— Bronze   ———————— Silver   ———————— Gold

The NNAS Navigator Awards relate to navigation skills rather than altitude

Gold Navigator Award

Open country and intricate terrain in mountainous country with few man-made features but excluding routes that require scrambling, rock climbing or rope-work skills.

Steep ground, where a slip might result in a fall, should be avoided. Navigation will require the application of skills learned at Bronze and Silver levels applied to more complex terrain. It will also focus on the use of subtle contour features and constant map contact where appropriate.

Interpretation of Award Levels

It is important to understand that the Award levels correspond purely with a progression of navigation skills and techniques with no specific relationship to altitude. The diagram above shows routes at Bronze, Silver and Gold levels in a single area at or around an altitude of 200 metres.

Many high mountain walks could be undertaken by holders of the Silver Navigator Award with care taken in poor visibility. Gold Navigator provides the skills to walk confidently in most conditions.

The Users of Land Navigation Skills

Land navigation skills are used not only for walking but also in several sports such as:

- Fell running
- Mountain marathons
- Competitive orienteering
- Adventure racing
- Mountain biking
- Ski touring

It is useful for a tutor to appreciate and learn about the needs of the various sports to broaden their approach to course delivery.

The extremes in the application of navigation skills are arguably walking and orienteering. Differences will relate to the specific demands of the activities, the routes to be followed and personal preference. The requirements in other sports will generally lie between these two extremes.

Walking

People who walk in the countryside probably do so for exercise, relaxation, to see the views and to enjoy the company of other people. There will generally be no need for high speed navigation decisions. Walks often follow obvious features for long distances meaning that maps can sometimes be put away.

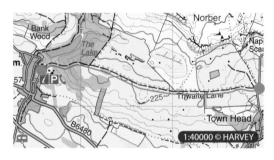

A simple route easily navigable by walkers from memory

Some walks, however, will involve complex footpath networks in rural areas, farmland and forest. Other walks may involve intricate terrain with complex contour detail. Any walk may involve bad weather or poor visibility. In such instances, maintaining constant map contact will generally be useful.

Orienteering

Orienteering is a competitive sport where the winner achieves the fastest time over a set course. Spending more time on navigation or choosing less optimal routes than a fellow competitor may result in a lower placing in the results. Minimising the time taken influences orienteering navigation styles.

Serious orienteers maintain map contact for much of the time. They use collecting and catching features to a greater extent than is necessary for many walks as a means of confirming accuracy and to avoid major errors. On the way to a control, they will study the map for the next leg while on the move and memorise at least the first part of the outgoing route to avoid wasting time while making a route choice.

In orienteering, controls in the harder events are often placed in obscure positions on small contour features in contrast to the more obvious targets and features generally used by walkers.

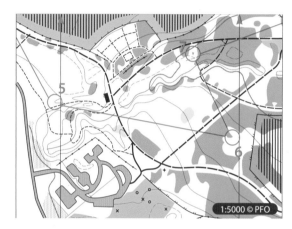

Orienteering controls sited away from main routes in intricate terrain require constant map contact

In essence, the orienteer's approach to navigation is not entirely essential for walking. An inexperienced walker, however, may benefit from the orienteering approach until attaining confidence in themselves.

Other Sports

In the sports mentioned previously, the participant will be moving at higher speeds than walkers. In some, the hands will be required to hold activity equipment. This will influence the manner in which navigational skills and techniques are applied e.g. a mountain biker has to ride the bike and view the terrain ahead of them continually. Any navigation decisions are likely to be made during occasional stops and the route ahead memorised.

In fell running, races often use the same route from year to year. Common practice is to reconnoitre the route in advance and learn the best route by heart. Map reading and navigation solutions are generally made ahead of the event except in poor visibility.

Learning Outcomes & Tutor Requirements

	Bronze	Silver	Gold Training	Gold Assessment
learning outcomes	To be able to plan & follow routes in the countryside using paths & tracks	To be able to plan & follow routes in the countryside away from paths & tracks	To be able to plan & follow routes in any open countryside, hill or forest environment	
minimum tutor competence* *tutors to work within the remit of their own award*	Girl Guide Walk Leader Level 3 Certificate in Basic Expedition Leadership	Walking Group Leader Mountain Leader Hill & Moorland Leader Award	Walking Group Leader Mountain Leader Hill & Moorland Leader Award	As for Gold Training plus experience of assessing on Hill & Moorland Leader Award/ML courses Statement of competence to confirm equivalent experience
tutor/student ratio for training & assessment	1:6 maximum	1:6 maximum	1:4 maximum	1:4 maximum
minimum course duration**	12 hrs minimum over 2 days Assessment included or at a later date as appropriate	12 hrs minimum over 2 days Assessment included or at a later date as appropriate	12 hrs minimum over 2 days Assessment at a later date	As appropriate up to 6 hrs
assessment distances	3-5km depending on terrain	5-8km depending on terrain		6-10km depending on terrain

*Other Leader Awards

Acceptance of other leader awards will be considered on a case by case basis.

**Minimum Course Duration

The minimum course durations are suggested for candidates with previous experience. Other candidates may need additional time.

Principles of Effective Teaching

The Planning and Delivery Process

Navigation comprises various skills and techniques which need to be appropriately selected to solve specific problems of how to get from one place to another. A technique will invariably use multiple skills and each skill will encompass several elements. The complex nature of navigation means that teaching requires considerable thought and planning coupled with imaginative exercises in order to implement an effective learning process.

Evaluating the subsequent effectiveness of the process is equally important. If a session was particularly successful, could the methods used be applied to other exercises? If a session was less effective than desired, why? If an idea didn't seem to work, does it simply need tweaking to make it better? Would it have worked with a different age group? Only by constant reflection will a tutor become truly effective at delivery.

Teach Outdoors Where Possible

It is preferable to teach outdoors from the outset to permit learning in a realistic environment, coupled with frequent and relevant practical work. By introducing topics only as and when needed, learning can take place in small and gradual stages. Through this process, participants will more readily assimilate the information which has been delivered.

Through the outdoor approach, the tutor can create an atmosphere which is highly motivating and which encourages the student to remain both focussed and enthusiastic. This handbook has been produced to aid tutors in developing this process. Even topics such as safety, access and conservation can largely be discussed outdoors.

Classroom sessions have their place, especially for small elements which are less suited to outdoor tuition. It is recommended that they are short, concise and at relevant times. A late afternoon or evening indoor session, for example, enables the information presented to be related to the daytime practical work for added effect.

Course Delivery

Course Duration and Previous Experience

The minimum course duration suggested in hours for each of the Awards should only be considered for students with significant walking experience who wish to learn to navigate for themselves. Complete beginners or college students who have never walked in the country before will generally need additional course time.

Teach Only the Award Syllabus Content

The syllabus has been carefully formulated by experienced practitioners to allow learning in sensible stages, without unnecessary overload for students. If the syllabus has been fully covered it will generally be preferable to allocate remaining time to reinforcement exercises rather than additional topics.

Teach Personal Competence Only

There should be no element of competition, or of tuition in leadership skills. The Awards are aimed only at personal competence in navigation.

Develop Self Confidence

The aim of NNAS Awards is to empower Award holders to undertake walks on a self-led basis. It is implicit, therefore, that tutors should try to provide opportunities for participants to take responsibility for making navigational decisions during the course.

Equip All Students with Map and Compass

Students will learn most effectively by having their own map and compass. Sharing equipment diminishes the learning opportunities. It is also useful to have a pointing device in order to indicate map positions clearly to the tutor e.g. compass corner.

Maps may need to be weather proofed with a map case or polythene bag though Harvey maps are printed on water resistant paper. Full size laminated maps are waterproof but cumbersome to handle.

The compass should be of the protractor type (Suunto, Silva, etc).

The map should preferably be carried in the hand so that it can be conveniently orientated at decision points. The map can be in a map case but without the cord attached to anything.

The compass should be to hand so that it can be used as a unit with the map. It could be attached by a cord to a rucsac strap, wrist or external pocket.

From a safety point of view, avoid having map and compass on long cords around the neck.

Use a Variety of Maps and Terrain

Students need to use a variety of maps so that they can appreciate the advantages and disadvantages of each type. They can also learn that skills are mostly transferable between the different map types.

A tutor should use varied terrain suited to the technique or skill being taught.

Use Logical Progressions

A new skill or technique is generally best introduced so that it follows on naturally from a student's existing knowledge. The individual steps of each new idea are also best introduced in a logical order.

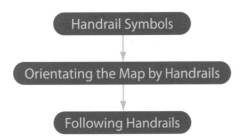

Use of Terminology

Tutors should use terminology consistently in order to make explanations as clear as possible e.g. use either 'collecting feature' or 'check point', not both.

The terms Skill, Technique and Strategy are used in this book as follows:

A *Skill* is a fundamental, mechanical process which can be learned by repetition e.g. setting a bearing on a compass.

A *Technique* is a combination of skills selected for a specific situation based on an analysis of the issues involved e.g. aiming off to find a stream junction.

A *Strategy* is a structured plan of the skills, techniques and terrain interpretation that will be required to navigate a whole leg.

Teach in Gradual Stages

People generally learn best if a complex skill or technique is broken down into gradual steps. However, a holistic demonstration or explanation of the final objective beforehand can sometimes be helpful.

Use Self-Learning Techniques where Possible

Whenever possible, aim to guide students towards formulating their own solutions. Encouraging a self thinking process is fundamental in formulating good personal strategies.

Involve All Students for All of the Time

Plan practical exercises so that all students can be engaged throughout a session. This ensures that constant learning or consolidation takes place. Preplanned extension exercises are useful to occupy fast learners but they should be within the syllabus.

Allow Students to Make Mistakes

Learning from mistakes is valuable experience. Recognising that a mistake has been made is, in any case, an important aspect of navigation as even the best navigators can occasionally suffer a lapse of concentration. Mistakes sometimes provide realistic opportunities to teach relocation techniques.

Evaluate Student Performance

It is good practice to review student progress continually in order to highlight areas that require further tuition or clarification. A useful approach is to begin by encouraging students to evaluate their own performance at the end of each exercise. Tutors can add to student comments as appropriate.

Understand the Nature of Navigation

Participants should understand that navigation consists of three principal elements: Route Planning, Route Following and Route Checking as a safeguard against human error or distraction. Re-planning the route while on the move may well be an inevitable outcome of the above process.

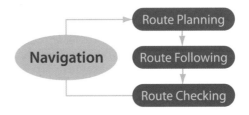

Choose and Plan a Whole Walk

From studying the map, students should be able to choose a whole walk and assess whether they have the navigational skills to tackle it.

The student should be able to break down the whole route into several legs and determine that it can be achieved within the time available.

Related Topics

Related topics (e.g. Access & Conservation, Safety, Emergency Procedures) should be covered as listed in the syllabus. Sources for appropriate information are listed in the Resources section.

A Staged Approach to Tutoring Navigation

Award	Stage	Skill/Technique
B R O N Z E	1	Identify common handrail symbols. Orientate the map against handrails Use an orientated map to follow handrails. Maintain position on the map General map symbols. Use collecting and catching features to aid navigation Estimate distance using grid squares. Use 4 & 6 figure grid references Estimate short distances by eye e.g. 100m = a football pitch length. Estimate the time needed to walk a specific horizontal distance Measure short distances on the ground using double pacin Have a simple understanding of scales e.g. 4cm = 1km at 1:25,000
	2	Differentiate between uphill and downhill on the map by reference to contours Recognise prominent hills, valleys, cols, ridges, and spurs on map and ground Orientate the map against major ground features Orientate the map against a compass needle Use an orientated map to check the direction of handrails
S I L V E R	3	Set a compass bearing from map to ground Use a compass to follow bearings accurately across open ground over short legs Measure distances with reasonable accuracy by double pacing and timing Estimate the time needed for height gain
	4	Use major landforms (hills, ridges, spurs, valleys) as a means of navigation Identify smaller contour features on map and ground e.g. re-entrants, small hills Use aiming off to reach a target on a linear feature Identify the most appropriate route where more than one option is available Use coarse navigation and collecting features to locate an attack point From an attack point use fine navigation to locate a target
G O L D	5	Use landform features as the prime navigation method Use intricate contour detail to aid route finding Use compass bearings to follow a route accurately over intricate terrain Deviate briefly from a route to avoid impassable terrain without losing accuracy Measure longer distances on the ground with reasonable accuracy by timing Measure shorter distances on the ground with reasonable accuracy by pacing
	6	Select the most appropriate strategy for a navigational leg Adjust pace to suit the difficulty of the terrain Take a compass bearing from ground to map Use back bearings and transits to confirm the current position Use 'aspect of slope' as an aid to relocation
	7	Navigate to features in intricate and difficult terrain Follow routes which require complicated navigation over long distances

This table summarises the NNAS approach to tutoring the content of the Navigator Awards. It provides a working model to be used in consultation with the syllabus and sample teaching exercises. Less than ideal circumstances might influence the actual tutoring approach used.

At each stage students should be able to:

• Master the content of the current stage before moving on to the next stage.

• Plan a route and explain the factors considered in choosing it.

• Accurately and safely follow a route.

• Select and apply relevant navigation techniques.

• Demonstrate relocation techniques appropriate to their skill level.

• Show awareness of safety and environmental issues.

Overview of Tutoring Skills

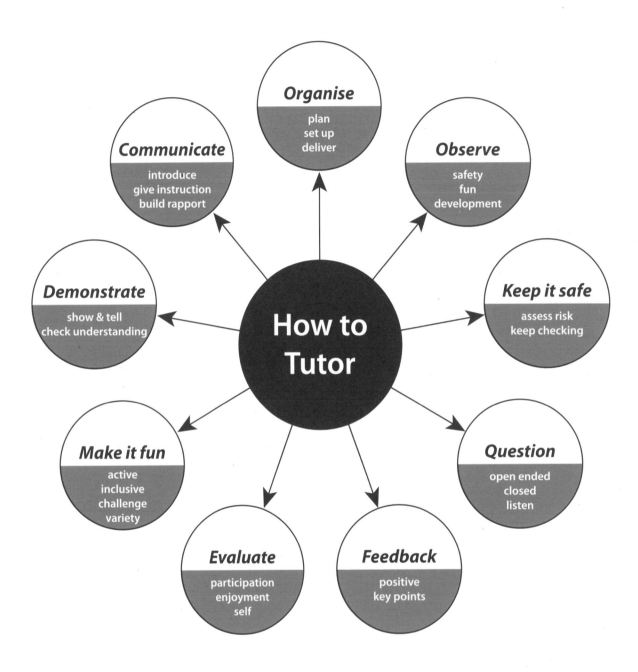

The preceding content details the demanding and complex nature of good tutoring practice. The diagram above provides a quick reminder of the key processes to aid the planning of courses.

Based on a 'How to Coach' diagram by British Orienteering.

Teaching Theory Indoors

Not all aspects of the NNAS Awards Syllabus can be conveniently taught outdoors. It is also inevitable that poor weather conditions will occasionally result in some aspects of outdoor work being taught indoors prior to outdoor practical work.

Teaching indoors requires as much thought and planning as outdoor sessions to provide maximum benefit for students. Remember that they have come to learn rather than to listen to the tutor talk!

The following principles should be considered:

Keep Talking to a Minimum
A good starting point is aiming to restrict talking to a maximum of one minute before involving students in some form of practical activity. It is possible to transmit a considerable amount of information in a minute and students may struggle to remember what has been said unless the talking is backed up with meaningful practical work.

Practical activity could be looking at points on an environmental leaflet; doing a map-related exercise; group discussion of a topic; etc.

Try to Develop a Two-Way Process
A useful way to maintain interest is to deliver in a style that requires responses from participants e.g.

- Ask open ended questions rather than ones that simply require yes or no answers.
- Allow students with previous experience to contribute their knowledge.
- Set tasks that require a response or outcome from participants on completion.
- Set tasks that require students to interact with each other.

A two-way approach helps to show students that the tutor is interested in their progress and provides a useful means for tutors to assess understanding. It is also a useful technique for assessment.

Use Research Tasks as a Vehicle for Learning
Asking students to find simple information from leaflets, books, websites, etc encourages self-learning and offers respite from listening to a tutor.

Change Topics at Regular Intervals
Labouring on one topic for a lengthy period can be tiresome for students. If practicable, covering just part of a topic with the remainder left until a later stage can sometimes be beneficial.

Choose Visual Aids Carefully
A good visual aid can reduce the need for talking, promote discussion and impact positively on the learning process. Real objects rather than images can create greater interest and opportunities for hands-on experiences. Looking at the group's own equipment can be a good way to achieve this.

Before using OHP's or Power Point consider whether there is an alternative. If it really is necessary to use such facilities, ensure they are designed to promote group involvement and discussion. Good slides will be mostly graphics-based and contain minimal text or no text at all. A good Power Point should support a training session rather than be the training session.

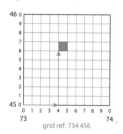

6-figure Grid References

grid ref: 734 456

A useful Power Point slide

Power Point is best used in short bursts followed with ongoing practical work. Occasionally a few good slides can be useful to reinforce some aspects of practical work undertaken beforehand.

In the event of poor weather, a selection of carefully chosen photographs to project on to a screen can provide a useful means of covering related topics such as safety, environmental issues, weather, etc.

Theory Should Relate to Practical Work
For maximum effect, wherever possible try to relate any indoor theory either to something which is about to be practised or to something which has recently been covered in a practical session.

Theory presented in relation to practical work may be more meaningful and easier to understand. It is also more likely to be remembered.

Try to Provide Support Materials
The tutor is likely to transmit a great deal of information. It is useful if handouts and leaflets can be supplied to students to help with retention of the key issues.

Planning a Walk

For the independent walker, the ability to plan and execute a whole walk is an essential element of enjoying the outdoor experience - the essence of the National Navigation Award Scheme. Equally, there is little point in learning navigation skills without the ability to plan and execute an overall route. At each Award level sufficient time should therefore be allocated to the issues involved in walk planning.

Step 1 - Set Criteria for Your Walk

- Desired duration.

- Personal physical limits.

- Overall walk objectives - ridge walk, valley walk, circular/linear/out-and-back walk, etc.

- Attractiveness and interest of walk.

- An adequate level of challenge (not all people want a leisurely walk).

- Stay on paths or within open access land.

- Personal responsibilities in relation to the type of land being used e.g. Countryside Code, Scottish Access Code, environmental issues.

Step 2 - Devise a Route Planning Process

- Choose the most suitable map for the walk.

- Scan area of walk for attractive route sections and places of interest.

- Connect up various sections to create a likely complete route, using trial and error as necessary, and considering the above walk criteria.

Students could work individually or in pairs to choose any route that seems suitable. Routes can be reviewed by students talking through their chosen routes with the tutor and colleagues.

Step 3 - Check and Adjust the Route

- Estimate walk duration. Emphasize that accuracy will develop from experience.

- Does the walk meet its original objectives?

- Is the walk sufficiently satisfying, attractive, challenging, etc?

- Is the walk within personal physical limits. Consider at what stage to include demanding sections depending on fitness, experience and motivation.

- Does the walk take account of the weather forecast? Can the route be successfully navigated in poor visibility, strong winds, etc? Can it be walked in reverse if necessary? Can all sections of the route be followed after prolonged, heavy rain - water hazards?

- Are there escape routes and the potential for shortening the route in case of problems?

- Logistics - parking place, transport timings, lunch stop, etc.

The checking process may lead to route adjustments followed by rechecking before a finalised route is formulated.

Step 4 - Recording the Route

There a number of methods:

- Route Card - has these benefits:

    Good for novices.

    Brings in many skills.

    Divides the walk into achievable chunks.

    Can be left with a third party for safety.

- Photocopy the route and then highlight it.

- Print from a digital mapping system.

- Mark up a laminated map with a permanent marker (wash off with methylated spirit).

- Consider alternatives for recording a route – long hand descriptive text, highlighting and annotating on a photocopy of the map, etc.

With sufficient experience, detailed route recording may become less essential with only a brief list of locations and grid references along the route left behind for safety purposes.

Step 5 - Replanning on the Walk

- Discuss the need for this and the skills needed to perform it.

    e.g. Having a simple way of measuring the length of the new route out in the field and doing the necessary mental arithmetic.

- When might a change of route be necesssary or desirable?

    e.g. Route difficult to complete in wind, cold and rain; route cut off by flooded river; bridge has been washed away; change in party mood or objectives.

Establish a Routine

Early in learning to navigate it is important to establish a sound routine. For example:

- Where am I?

- Where do I want to get to?

- How am I going to get there?

- What is it going to be like along the way?

- What will I see along the way?

- How will I know when I've got there?

This underpins all navigation. At Bronze level the skills that can be applied to the routine are the basic ones. Subsequent levels introduce additional skills and strategies to add to the navigator's toolkit, thus enabling reliable navigation in ever more challenging environments.

Occupying the Whole Group

Teaching navigation requires considerable thought and planning to provide maximum benefit for all course members. If a single student navigates a leg while the others simply follow then the followers may learn very little from the experience. Avoiding this kind of situation means planning exercises that can simultaneously engage all students.

Besides the learning benefits of this approach, the use of such techniques can add a degree of novelty and amusement which helps maintain the group's interest and motivation in a session.

Exercises of this nature also encourage the student to study the map more carefully and identify the key information needed for following a route reliably.

Whole Group Exercises

Mystery Destination
Ask a single student to navigate to a specific control (see p20 for usage of terms) which is unknown to the rest of the group. Ask the remaining students to follow the navigator and identify the route taken on the map.

On arrival at the target, ask the students individually to indicate the route on their map using a pointing device. This avoids the use of speech so that other students cannot overhear.

Check Points
Ask the whole group to follow a planned route. Stop at intervals and ask each student individually to point to where they are on the map. A pointing device will be helpful.

Confirm the Control Position
At each control ask all students to provide two or more pieces of evidence that confirm its location e.g. nearby features, direction of line features, time taken, relief, etc.

Change Navigator
Allocate a new navigator at intervals without telling the new navigator where they are and without the group knowing who will be asked next.

Remembering Features
From a known location, nominate one student to navigate a route to a control which is unknown to the remainder of the group. The other students follow without a map. When the control is reached, allow each student to view their map and ask them in turn to point to the appropriate position.

This encourages the following students to memorise the key features around them on the ground. This can be a valuable process for acquiring evidence for relocation in the event of a navigation error.

Individual and Sub-group Exercises

Map Memory
The navigator is allowed to study the map for a given leg in order to identify and memorise key features along the route. Navigation subsequently proceeds from memory only, with the map taken away. This fosters the identification of collecting features, catching features and timing before embarking on a leg. It also develops simplification skills and route finding without continual reference to the map.

It may be feasible to use the same exercise with a whole group.

Limit Map Use
Limit the number of times on a leg the navigator or group can look at the map.

Navigate by Instructions Only
Working in pairs, the tutor indicates to one person in each pair (without the other's knowledge), a clearly identifiable and not too distant control (1km max). This person then provides three instructions to the navigator that should enable them to find it, without the navigator knowing what it actually is. Compasses can be retained but the tutor should not mention them or imply that they can be used. It may be feasible to allocate a different target to each pair.

When the navigator thinks the first control has been reached, the partner (without confirming accuracy) returns the map. The navigator then proceeds to a second control (previously defined by the tutor as a group assembly point) about 1km away. This can provide some useful relocation practice if the first control was incorrectly found!

No Compass Allowed
On a clear day, following a route in open country without a compass (taken away by tutor) is valuable at Silver and Gold levels in order to encourage route finding by terrain features, particularly large ones. This, too, is useful for developing relocation skills.

Follow the Line of a Contour
Navigate along the line of a contour from a known position. This encourages concentration on adjacent features or fine contour detail in order to maintain the correct height. Any technique (except the use of

altimeters) including use of a compass, is allowed.

Where's the Path!

In an area with a path depicted on the map but not visible on the ground, the student is asked to follow the line of the path accurately. This can be a useful exercise in farmland where infrequently used routes may not be visible as paths. In this case, navigation by field shapes and stiles is often the solution.

In hills and mountains, walkers sometimes create additional paths by following a different line to the one shown on the map e.g. to get closer to the edge of a hill for a better view. In some cases the original path disappears through lack of use. Following the line of the original path in these circumstances may provide an interesting navigation exercise.

Exercises of this nature highlight that maps cannot always be relied upon to reflect the current situation on the ground. Even rights of way may be indistinct. Inexperienced walkers can be unnerved if a path is not visible and may need reassurance that following such routes is permissible.

Leap Frog

This exercise, detailed in navigation books, can be used to maintain direction on a compass bearing in open country in poor visibility. It can be used during a course to demonstrate the amount of time needed to implement such techniques, not to mention the inconvenience of using them.

The Navigation Trio

Split the group into threes. Within each group, one student uses a compass, one paces and one identifies ground features. This is a good opportunity to practise a single skill while moving along a leg.

Route Cards Only

Navigate a leg using a route card only. Students are advised of the exercise in advance and given an opportunity to produce their own route card.

This exercise is primarily for fun and may produce route cards which are too detailed for general use. It does, however, provide a focal point for discussing what information is really needed on a card.

Loop Courses

Select a relatively small area which is within the competence level of all students. It is useful if the area has clearly identifiable boundary features such as roads or major tracks to prevent students from accidentally going astray. From a static base devise three separate loop courses. Ideally the base will afford a good view over the area to be used. Each loop could require the same skills and techniques or

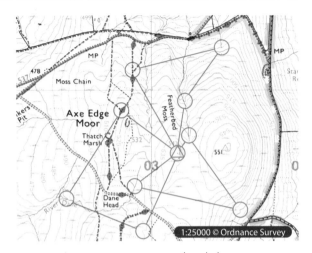

Loop courses can occupy the whole group and develop confidence in solo navigation

they could be varied to provide a wider range of practice. Such exercises provide a useful first step in the development of confidence for solo navigation.

Each control will need a coded marker such as an orienteering kite or a homemade equivalent. Each marker needs to be fitted with a different crayon or orienteering punch that can be used to prove that the site has been visited. Students will require some form of recording device such as a grid drawn on a small piece of card. They will also need a list of the ID codes in order to know that they have reached the correct location. Students can tackle the loops individually or in pairs, returning to base each time before being sent off on a different loop. All control markers should be collected in when the exercise is finished for environmental reasons. Sending students to collect them provides further navigation practice and can save time.

Tutors should remain at the base to monitor the exercise and review with students the techniques and strategies that they used for each leg.

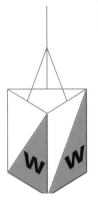

A control punch was once used to confirm visits to control sites at orienteering events. They have generally been superceded by electronic recording systems.

An orienteering control marker kite (right) is used to confirm arrival at the correct location.

Both items can be used on solo navigation routes during NNAS courses but cheap, homemade substitutes are just as viable.

Maps for NNAS Courses

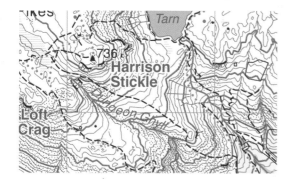

HARVEY 1:25000 Maps

These use 15m contours which means there are fewer lines to obscure other detail. Grey contours indicate rocky ground/outcrops which further adds to the clarity of these maps. Intermediate contour lines are used where necessary to pick out land forms missed by standard contours.

Cultivated land is distinguished from open fell/moorland. Wet conditions underfoot (marsh, peat hags) are shown.

The strong colours used are good for legibility in poor light/weather conditions. The maps are printed on water resistant material which adds to their durability.

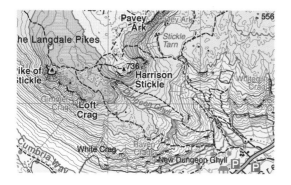

HARVEY 1:40000 Maps

These maps offer the same basic characteristics as the 1:25000 maps and are also printed on water resistant materials.

They use a coloured banding system to indicate height ranges in addition to the contour lines themselves. This assists with the visualisation of relief shape.

Some maps show complex summit areas as a separate inset at a larger scale.

OS 1:25000 Explorer Maps

These show considerable detail which can be useful in intricate terrain. Of particular value is the depiction of walls and fences in all areas which can simplify navigation particularly through farmland if paths are indistinct. Congested detail in some areas can make relief interpretation difficult through contour detail being obscured.

The tendency to print maps on both sides together with their large sheet size can make them cumbersome and inconvenient to use particularly in windy conditions.

OS 1:50000 Landranger Maps

These show less detail than OS 1:25000 maps, with an absence of walls and fences but have several advantages including single sided printing.

For a given sheet size, they show a larger area than the equivalent 1:25000. This can be useful on longer walks as it lessens the need to refold the map.

In mountain and moorland areas they are often clearer to read than OS 1:25000 maps and they are usually less cluttered though they lack detail which would be useful to walkers.

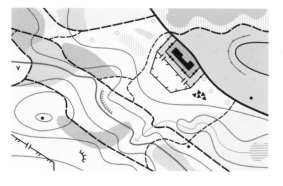

Orienteering Maps

Orienteering maps show considerable detail in a small area. This allows intense navigation practice in the time available. The most readily accessible areas are at Permanent Orienteering Courses. Scales range from 1:2000 - 1:10000. Locations are listed on club websites accessed via the British Orienteering website.

Competition maps at scales of 1:10000 and 1:15000 may offer value for Gold courses but not all are available for general use.

Orienteering maps vary considerably in nature and it is wise to check that a particular map is suitable for the desired purpose.

Principles of Map Use

Map Choice

Students at all levels should experience a range of walking map types and scales to aid understanding of the issues involved in selecting an appropriate map for a particular walk. Orienteering maps can be useful for training but their use is not compulsory and the main emphasis should be on walking maps.

Carrying a range of maps on a training session will allow students to contrast navigation with specific types to suit varying circumstances at different stages. This should show that map choice influences the navigation techniques that can be used.

Maps with field boundaries aid navigation in intricate farmland. Knowing on which side of a boundary a path lies can be particulary helpful.

1:25000 © Ordnance Survey

Tutors should discuss map choice and highlight the implications and limitations of each type of map through practical exercises.

- Smaller scale maps allow the eye to view a greater area at one time than large scale maps. They may offer greater clarity through being less cluttered. Smaller scales offer advantages for general relief interpretation over large areas.

- Routes in intricate farmland may need a map that shows field boundaries. Maps without them may require a higher level of initiative or relief interpretation.

- Major, well-trodden routes may be adequately served by a 1:50000 or 1:40000 scale map.

- 1:25000 maps generally show a higher level of information about vegetation.

- The presence of administrative (e.g. parish) boundary lines and other items that obscure vital detail may require the use of a clearer map.

- Intricate terrain may require a map with detailed contours for micro navigation.

- A poor visibility forecast may require a detailed map for micro navigation in the event that a route is lost.

- 1:25000 maps can require refolding during a walk which can be tricky in bad weather.

- A map type that shows a route on a single sheet

may be more convenient than one that requires two or more sheets.

Smaller scale maps generally provide better clarity for easier interpretation of general relief.

1:50000 © Ordnance Survey

Map Accuracy

Students should be aware that some areas of a map can be inaccurate through factors such as:

- Man-made changes since map publication

- Limitations of surveying & cartography

Inexperienced walkers can be unnerved when a map does not portray what is on the ground and will need guidance in how to handle such situations. Tutors should find areas with accuracy problems and examine solutions through practical exercises. Typical problems are:

- Paths may have been realigned, or disappeared through lack of use.

- In popular areas there may be more paths on the ground than the map shows.

- New bridges may have appeared or original bridges removed or repositioned.

- Roads may have been realigned especially in areas with new bypasses.

- Buildings may have been built or taken down.

- Forests/woodland may have been reduced or extended and new tracks added.

Accuracy problems can be minimised by using the latest edition of a map and students can be asked to locate the edition date. However the map may state that the latest revisions only apply to certain aspects of the map such as main roads. Using an outdated map is often practicable but may require higher levels of observation and initiative.

Some 1:25000 maps can also offer good clarity to help with interpretation of both general and intricate relief.

1:25000 © HARVEY

Coping With Inaccuracies

If a walker maintains frequent map contact but finds a situation that appears incorrect, it may be an inaccuracy in the map. The solution lies in remaining confident and using a sensible strategy e.g.

Woodland areas are notorious for changes to vegetation and tracks that can quickly cause a map to become outdated. Extra care with navigation will often be needed in such areas.

1:25000 © HARVEY

- Orientate the map with a compass.
- Check that distant features correspond with those on the map.
- Move a short distance off route and check the features against the map.
- Move a short distance ahead or back along the route and check the features against the map.

This approach should enable most map inaccuracy problems to be identified. In more problematic cases relocation techniques (p31) may be required.

Enlarged Maps

An enlarged map can provide a clearer view of the map information. Remember, however, that any enlargement is a copy of a normal map and is thus subject to copyright issues.

It is preferable to use normal map scales for both training and assessment courses as that is what walkers will generally use and they need to learn to cope with problems encountered.

A 1:50000 extract enlarged to 1:25000 for increased clarity. In particular, an enlargement may make it easier to see that some contours have been omitted on very steep terrain.

© Ordnance Survey

Ordnance Survey OpenData

OpenData is a facility provided by Ordnance Survey allowing free use of a limited range of OS mapping. 1:25000 and 1:50000 maps are specifically excluded

from this arrangement. Mapping which is available through OpenData at the present time is unlikely to be of use to NNAS tutors for running courses leading to Navigator Awards. Some free street mapping may be useful for Outdoor Discovery Award courses. See www.ordnancesurvey.co.uk for current information.

Map Copying

It is useful to advise students on the legalities of map copying, especially if copies are used during a course. Promoting illegal copying of maps, either inadvertently or otherwise, must be avoided at all costs. Tutors should be aware that penalties for copyright infringements are usually very high.

Photocopying maps is illegal unless it is performed under licence. Printing from software based sources such as Anquet Maps or Memory Map, in situations that involve financial gain, requires a commercial licence. Tutors who charge for NNAS courses should seek appropriate advice from the software supplier. An OS or HARVEY licence would also be required.

HARVEY offers a licence scheme for individuals, organisations and commercial enterprises and may provide this at discount to registered NNAS tutors. OS has a variety of annual map copying licences available for varying circumstances.

Many local authorities have a blanket licence for copying OS maps and maps based on OS mapping such as orienteering maps and school grounds maps. Where tutors have access to this via schools, colleges, etc, they should obtain the licence number (typically of the form LAxxxxxx) from the authority and ensure it is displayed on the copied map along with the standard OS Copyright text. The resulting copies may only legally be used if working for or on behalf of the authority concerned.

Many orienteering maps and school grounds maps are based on OS mapping and are thus subject to OS royalty payments via British Orienteering. If maps have been obtained through a visitor centre or club then royalties should have been paid by the club. Buying a single map to photocopy is simply illegal. It would breach the club's copyright and leave the tutor personally liable for payment of OS royalties.

Some school grounds maps may have been wholly produced from an original survey by the mapper concerned. With their permission, the maps can be freely copied without reference to external agencies.

Equipment for NNAS Courses

Compasses for Walkers

Students should know that compasses for walkers from reputable manufacturers generally have the same level of needle alignment accuracy. All the models featured are of a premium quality, but still provide value beyond price, offering a choice of sizes and features to match the requirements of a wide selection of users. All models have varying romer scales.

Basic Compass

Suunto A-10 CM

A premium quality but still economically priced model, ideal for less experienced walkers, groups etc., using bearings over relatively short distances. Has a fixed declination adjustment scale.

Compass with Additional Features

Suunto A-30 CM

Still economically priced, but with the extra features of a luminous bezel, ideal in dim or dark conditions, and a magnifier – excellent for finding that essential detail on the map. Has a fixed declination adjustment scale. This model will suit those working to a budget, whilst meeting most navigational requirements.

Compasses for the More Experienced User and the Traveller

Suunto M-3 CM and M-3G

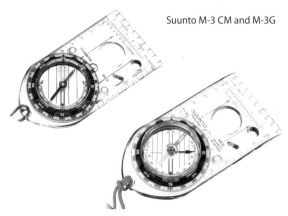

Models for the adventurer, traveller & those requiring that 'quick response'. The longer base plate provides an easier 'on map' routing between points, whilst the larger luminous bezel, great for use in the cold/with gloves, with degrees at base level, provides ease of use and legibility; plus silicon feet for non-slip map use, a magnifier and orienteering marker shapes.

The 'G' model adds the globally balanced needle for worldwide use and that comforting 'quick settle' of the needle; plus a clinometer and declination scales.

Mirror Compasses

Suunto MCA-D CM & MCB

Mirror compasses are an aid to navigation by using the compass features to align the route according to the map and sighting the features. The left model includes a luminous bezel and fixed declination marks. The model on the right floats – ideal for canoeing, and includes a safety whistle.

Suunto MC2-360-G-D-L

These are the adventurer professional mirror compass models. They include a larger base plate, with magnifier, whilst the larger luminous bezel, great for use in the cold/with gloves, with degrees at base level, provides ease of use and legibility, a clinometer and magnifier; plus silicon feet for non-slip map use, and declination adjustment scales.

The 'G' model adds the globally balanced needle for worldwide use, with its 'quick settling' feature.

Global Compasses

The earth's magnetic field has two influences on a compass needle:

Declination (magnetic variation) is the angle at which the needle aligns to true north.

Inclination is the vertical pull on the needle.

Both declination and inclination vary in different parts of the world and compensation must be made for them to ensure accurate compass readings.

Declination Compensation is made by the navigator each time a bearing is used. This will generally be based on information obtained from the map in use.

Inclination Compensation is made by the compass manufacturer in one of two ways. The needle can be balanced purely to suit a specific hemisphere of the world. For example a northern hemisphere balanced compass can only reliably be used in the northern hemisphere. Alternatively, a global compass would be designed with a "floating magnet" to enable accurate use anywhere in the world

The globally balanced models settle more quickly than standard models, which makes such a purchase worthwhile for more local use too, if your use is extensive, especially in more challenging terrain.

Sighting Compass

This model is the under mirror sighting compass, unique in style, use and robustness. A model favoured for military use in a number of countries. Sight across the top of the box using the gun-like sights and read the direction off the mirror beneath. The bezel housing includes an 'off-line' facility to enable obstacles to be by-passed, a clinometer and declination adjustment scales. Just slide the box closed for protection when not in use.
Available with or without the global needle system.

Suunto MB-6

Romer

A romer is a twin axis measuring device designed for use with a specific map scale. Each axis represents 1km with 10 divisions each representing 100m.

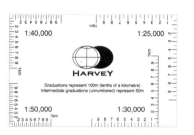

A multi-scale romer for independent use

Romers are sometimes included on compass base plates at various scales. They are also available as a separate tool which can be useful for teaching.

Romers are used as an aid for grid reference work. They are also used for accurate measurement of small distances. Their use is covered on p 24-25.

Altimeter

Altimeters are available as a totally independent device or inbuilt into wrist watches. To indicate altitude, most altimeters rely on atmospheric pressure which can vary considerably depending on the prevailing weather conditions. Getting reliable readings from an altimeter requires the user to recalibrate the device frequently at known heights.

Suunto Vector yellow wrist watch

GPS

The NNAS Navigator Awards exclude the use of electronic navigation aids. Rather they seek to introduce and develop traditional navigation skills. NNAS recommends that walkers should master at least the skills of the Silver Navigator Award before using GPS.

Satmap Active 12

GPS, in essence, is a means of indicating position and can indicate the direction of the next waypoint. However, the direction (bearing) indicated is a straight line that may not necessarily follow a safe or practicable route. The use of traditional map and compass skills alongside GPS is thus important.

Should students ask about GPS, tutors should advise that there are many different models with varying level of operational simplicity. Thorough research is advised prior to the purchase of such an instrument for personal use.

Illustrations courtesy of Suunto, Satmap and HARVEY

Tutoring the Skills of the Bronze Navigator Award

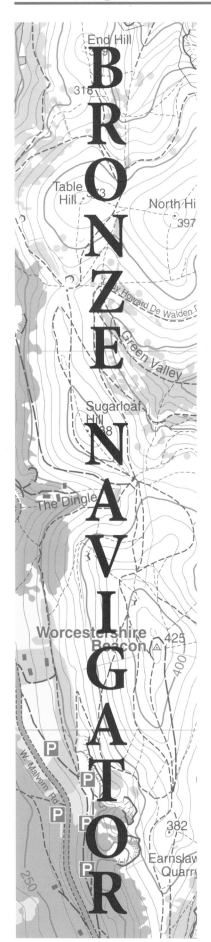

Bronze Navigator Award Syllabus

Minimum course duration is 2 days with at least 12 hours of tutor contact time. Additional time may be required for inexperienced candidates.

Maximum tutor/student ratio for training and assessment is 1:6.

The Learning Outcomes

On completion of the award participants will be able to plan and safely follow walks in the countryside, primarily on paths and tracks, through being able to:

* Navigate using a variety of maps and scales.

* Orientate the map using handrails, obvious point features and major land-forms.

* Use linear features (e.g. paths, tracks, clear boundaries) as handrails in simple navigation exercises.

* Relate prominent landforms such as large hills and valleys to corresponding contour information on the map.

* Orientate the map by aligning a compass needle against grid north and be aware that magnetic variation causes an inaccuracy.

* Use an orientated map to confirm direction of travel.

* Use clearly identifiable features to confirm position along the route and to recognise when the target has been overshot.

* Measure horizontal distance on the map and estimate distance on the ground using timing, pacing and simple visual judgements e.g.100m.

* Use 4 and 6 figure grid references with worded descriptions to define the position of a map feature and to locate a feature on the ground.

* Plan and implement simple routes and navigation strategies based on the above skills.

* Recognise a navigation error within a few minutes and apply simple reloca-tion techniques using handrails and prominent features.

* Demonstrate an awareness of local and national access issues, access legisla-tion, personal responsibilities and the Countryside Code.

* Demonstrate appropriate knowledge of walking equipment, safety equip-ment and emergency procedures.

Assessment Guidance Notes

* Assessment may take place immediately after training or on a separate occa-sion depending on the experience of the course members.

* Practical assessment should take place over a distance of 3 to 5km depend-ing on terrain.

* The route used should preferably have frequent changes in direction to assess map orientation skills and route following decisions.

* The route used should preferably facilitate the identification of obvious adja-cent point features and prominent landforms.

* Candidates should be assessed on their ability to navigate using a variety of simple line features in open countryside and/or woodland.

* Candidates should plan a safe walk of appropriate distance, explain the issues involved and estimate the time needed for a specific leg.

* Candidates should demonstrate an acceptable level of knowledge of the Countryside Code.

Choice of Areas for Tutoring & Walking

Guidance on the areas to be used for tutoring and practice exercises is provided within the Remit for Course Delivery on p1. Areas chosen should ideally permit plentiful and varied practice of skills.

Tutors should discuss in general terms typical regions, both locally and nationally, for which the Bronze Navigator Award skills are most appropriate, along with related issues such as:

- Avoidance of straying accidentally into areas which require navigational ability beyond the skills of the Bronze Navigator Award.

- Understanding that walking in inappropriate areas can make relocation problematic through the absence of adequate skills, especially in poor visibility.

- Recognising that straying into difficult terrain that is beyond their walking experience and ability can be dangerous with an increased risk of an accident, especially in poor visibility.

Stress that choice of areas used for the participant's own ventures is entirely their own responsibility.

Introducing the Map

Prior to tuition, a general introduction to the map with a brief outline of its content and features can be very useful. Learning how to unfold and refold the map at the beginning should save time later in the course. For most of the time, using the map as a book by flipping from section to section is preferable to completely unfolding it. It is worth mentioning how and why maps are sometimes inaccurate.

Map Symbols

Encourage students to learn just a few key symbols before commencing navigation i.e. paths & tracks, field boundaries, water features and buildings. Other symbols will lodge in the memory naturally by using them in the field. Less common symbols can be looked up in the legend as required.

A separate legend sheet can be useful as folded maps will generally prevent the legend from being conveniently on view. Legends can be downloaded from the HARVEY and OS websites. Copying a legend from a map for a group is technically illegal.

Comparing the legend against features on the ground for less common symbols should reinforce its value. Learning can be reinforced with flash cards by selecting just the cards which are appropriate for the skills being learned at any particular time.

Orientating the Map against Handrails

Competent walkers in Bronze terrain would mostly navigate against handrails and adjacent features. During the Bronze assessment, a candidate would certainly need to demonstrate the ability to do this.

Teaching map orientation with a compass from the outset will help to achieve accurate map orientation quickly. However, the student may then conclude that other methods are unnecessary.

Teaching orientation of the map against handrails at the very beginning introduces the skill in a realistic context. Progressing at a later stage to orientating the map with a compass in order to check a route direction is, again, realistic. In Bronze terrain, the compass would normally only be used as a check in a moment of uncertainty.

For those who struggle with orientation by handrails, hand-drawn diagrams of the junctions along the route, without the presence of other map features, may assist in focusing on handrails only.

Using a permanently orientated map is an orienteering technique that walkers may only need in very complex terrain. Students may, however, benefit from this approach until becoming confident. See Maintaining Position on the Map on p20.

Handrail Navigation

Handrails offer the basic framework for competent navigation. It is important that students appreciate their value even at Gold Navigator standard.

- Start by asking students to suggest ideas for simple ways of navigating.

  Develop their suggestions into the value of using handrails as a fundamental process.

- Select a relatively small area with lots of tracks and paths (preferably different kinds) and changes of direction (decision points). This will enable map orientation practice at frequent intervals, ideally every 5 minutes or so.

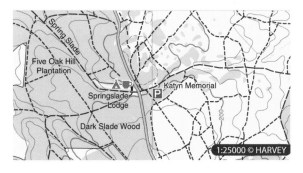

A small area with many path junctions enables frequent practice of map orientation and route finding decisions

After orientating the map, students should hold the map in front of them so that the path on the map points in the same direction as the intended route on the ground. The map then stays still and the body moves around it.

Move your body round the map!

Students who have difficulty with this can be asked to place their map on the floor in its correctly orientated position then walk around it until facing the direction of travel.

- If using students to lead, change the leader frequently, perhaps every 10 minutes or after no more than 3 changes of direction. Avoid using collecting features at this stage.

- If the area is fairly small with good boundaries, students could be sent on individual loops, returning to base after each one is completed.

- Repeat the exercise in an area which has other handrails such as fences, walls, streams, woodland boundaries, etc to develop awareness of other kinds of handrail. Introduce methods for maintaining position on the map.

Maintaining Position on the Map

In complex areas, it can sometimes be useful to have a continual awareness of position on the map in order to reduce the chance of making a mistake when following a route. A technique often used by orienteers is folding and thumbing the map. This entails folding the map so that only the immediate area is on view. The thumb is continually moved to the last known location and points along the route to be followed next. With a correctly orientated map, the thumb should always point straight ahead in relation to the ground.

Walkers are likely to use a full walker's map folded into a map case or similar. This results in an area of map which is generally too large for thumbing. For early exercises, a simple alternative is to use a pointing device. This should preferably be flat so that it can be held firmly against the map without slipping. The diagram shows how the pointer is realigned at each major change of direction. The route indicated by the red dotted line involves passing path junctions at A, B and C. These positions should be clearly identifiable locations at which to realign the pointing device to progressively maintain position on the map as the route is followed.

Position X lies between two path junctions at a point where the rightward tending path changes to a leftward tending path. This is another potential location at which to realign the pointing device.

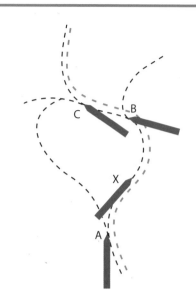

Ideally, the pointer will be realigned at every linear feature along the route where a change of direction is clearly identifiable on both map and ground.

Checking Route Finding Accuracy

The terms commonly used (and which are used in this book) in connection with route accuracy checks are:

- **Control**
  The start or finish of an individual leg or section

- **Collecting Feature**
  A feature that should be passed while walking along the leg

- **Catching Feature**
  A feature that helps to identify that the walker has strayed beyond the target control point

Alternative terminology is used by some tutors. Consistent use during a course is important to avoid confusion.

- Control: target, objective, destination

- Collecting feature: tick off feature, checking point

- Catching feature: stopping or overshoot feature

Catching and collecting features are important in order to verify the accuracy of route finding and to minimise the chances of going seriously astray.
Try to use relatively small areas with lots of features to facilitate intensive practice.

It is preferable to use routes with several decision points and several collecting features. Symbols on the map need to be recognised in advance then used to identify the features on the ground as they are encountered.

It is important to identify catching features for each leg where present.

In the absence of a reliable catching feature it may be possible to use a collecting feature as a substitute if it will be passed a short distance before the end of the leg.

Advise that an excessive number of collecting features are being used for learning purposes. For normal navigation, even just one obvious collecting feature may often be sufficient.

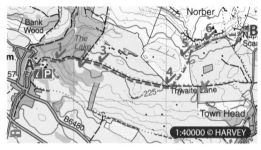

---- Route ✔Collecting feature ✘Catching feature

The example shows 6 collecting features:

1 - Two clear path bends.

2 - The track junction.

3 - The woods to the south.

4 - The wall end where the route turns north

5 - The wall corner

6 - Any of the crags to the north

The main catching features at the red cross are the wall running north and the strip of woodland runing south.

Distance Measurement

Distance and Accuracy
It is important to be realistic in respect of 'accurate' measurement in navigation. The instruments used to measure map distances may not be fully accurate. Neither is there any guarantee that the map itself is always absolutely accurate.

Ground measurement using pacing or timing is equally not wholly reliable. In particular, conditions underfoot, sloping ground and lack of practice can affect the stride length. With no reliable means of measuring walking speed, timing as a means of judging distance is never likely to be spot on.

A Realistic Approach to Accuracy
A sensible approach is to accept that measurement will never be fully accurate and to make decisions intelligently on that basis. Generally, most walkers will produce errors of less than 10%. The following strategy could thus be used:

On a leg estimated as 140 paces, a 10% error would translate to 14 paces. The target might, therefore, appear anywhere between 126 paces and 154 paces.

With timing, a 20 minute leg would translate to the target being between 18 and 22 minutes away.

At Bronze Navigator level, the expectation is that candidates should measure approximately rather than show a high degree of competence at this skill.

Measuring Distance on the Map

Tutors should introduce the common methods for measuring distance on the map.

- Grid squares and estimation by eye
- Ruler, romer or compass scale
- String
- Map measuring wheel

Stress that accuracy is not guaranteed. String, in particular, can be quite inaccurate in unskilled hands.

Measuring with Grid Squares
Grid squares offer a means for quickly estimating the rough length of a route or navigation leg. 100m subdivisions can be useful for greater accuracy or for estimating shorter distances. If accuracy is important, a physical measuring device may be preferable.

Visually estimating tenths of a grid square, with the presence of all the map information to confuse the issue, is not always easy. If the grid square is close to the edge of the map then the 100m divisions along the edge could be used as a reference.

Another method is to place a pointer or finger nail halfway along a square to create a mid-point reference position. The task is then reduced to estimating 1/5 of the space either side.

The diagonal of a grid square (approximately 1.4km) can also be a useful aid to estimating distance

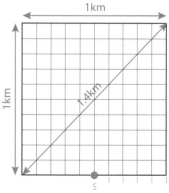

Using the mid-point to simplify estimation

Measuring Distance on the Ground

By Double Pacing

Pacing should be viewed as an introductory topic at Bronze level to be used in a low key way. Whilst not essential for navigation at this level, it provides a means of helping with visual distance judgement. By pacing, for example, 100m, students should correspondingly learn what 100m looks like on the ground.

Basic pacing is best learned on a stretch of horizontal ground over a 100m distance that has been pre-measured with a tape or road measuring wheel.

Encourage the use of a relaxed stride that can be repeated with reasonable reliability. Count double paces to reduce the amount of counting required.

Repeat the exercise two or three times and calculate an average figure. A second site could be used later to confirm the degree of accuracy maintained.

By Timing - The Timed Kilometre

Converting a map-measured distance into walking time is one way of judging distance. For the Bronze Navigator Award, only the time needed to cover a horizontal distance is necessary. A simple approach for a personal basis that avoids rules is as follows:

- The tutor finds a good track which is easy to follow and which offers a 1km section of flat terrain with clear start and finish points.

- Students are instructed to walk the kilometre at a steady pace that could be maintained all day and to record the time taken.

- On completion, students will each have an individual figure for estimating the time taken to walk a specific horizontal distance.

The practical nature of this approach creates an air of intrigue and provides students with a simple means of checking the figure to be used from time to time as their walking ability strengthens.

Avoid the height element at this stage as it is part of the Silver Navigator Award. Bronze Navigator Award holders should be using terrain where time for height gain is not important. If they wish to walk in hillier terrain they could increase the horizontal time by 10% to 20% if necessary.

Time-based Scales

Mathematics can be simplified or minimised via a time scale approach. A speed of 5km/hr equates to 12 min/km. On a 1:25000 map, 1km is 4cm. 1cm on the map thus equates to 3 minutes of walking time. A leg measured at 6cm would take 18 minutes.

Alternatively, a time scale could be constructed. The 2 minute graduation spacing in this instance is 6.66mm. Graphics software with an auto distribute facility is the easy way to achieve this. Such a scale could be designed to suit personal walking speed.

Walking speed 5km/hr with a 1:25000 map

Scales

Many people can be confused by the mathematics of fractional scales. Moving quickly on to the idea that '4cm on the map represents 1km on the ground' (or similar) is a far more practical and useful notion. That 1:25000 is twice as big in linear terms as 1:50000 can be shown quite simply by physically comparing the grid squares of the respective maps.

The practical implications of the various map scales are more significant than the scales themselves. Knowing, for example, that 1:25000 maps show more detail than 1:50000 maps is useful (see pages 13-14).

National Grid

Explain at an early stage that the national grid squares on maps are 1km along each edge. They have three major applications:

- Measuring or estimating distance on the map.

- Defining position on the map.

- A north reference line for compass work.

The first two applications require the ability to divide the edge of the square into 100m divisions. Doing this fluently may take a while to develop. A useful progression to minimise confusion would be:

- Using 4-figure grid references as a useful means of locating small areas on the map without the need to estimate 100m divisions.

- Roughly measuring distance on the map using whole grid squares only.

- Measuring linear distance on the map using grid squares and 100m divisions.

- 6-figure grid references.

Leaving 6-figure grid references until last ensures that students will already be equipped with the background knowledge to handle them.

Grid References

It is preferable to teach grid references in two stages; 4 figure first then 6 figure later.

4 Figure Grid References

Using 4 figure grid references on the first day of a course has several advantages:

- They are perfectly adequate in their own right for many situations. In the example below the location can be described as 'the trig station in grid square 7244'.

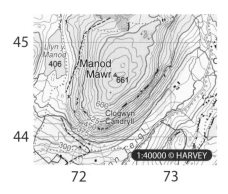

- Grid references describe positions using squares. With a 4 figure reference the square is actually visible on the map which admirably serves to illustrate and reinforce this principle. The intersecting lines which provide the basis for the grid reference are equally visible on the map and can be seen to be intersecting at the SW corner of the square.

- 4 figure grid references can easily be taught outdoors from an early stage as no estimating is required. This avoids the need for a prior classroom session.

- Along with a supportive description of an obvious feature in the square, a 4 figure grid reference is adequate for giving early teaching instructions. It also allows students to quickly focus on the area of map in use to facilitate efficient communications with tutors.

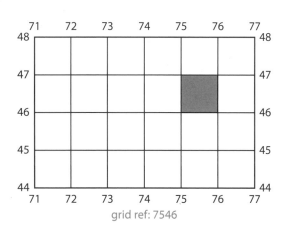

grid ref: 7546

Teaching 4 Figure Grid References

- The strength of 4 figure references is that they are simple and enable lots of practice in a short time to help remember how to do them without special rules.

- The tutor should stress that a grid reference is defined by two numbers associated with the vertical and horizontal lines that intersect at the SW corner of the square in question. The first number is shown on the bottom edge of the map and usually on the upper edge too. The second number is shown on the left hand edge of the map and usually on the right hand edge. Both numbers may be found within the map area itself on some maps.

- The learning jingles used as memory aids for grid references cannot generally be used with the figures along the top and right hand edges of the map so can be unhelpful. They can equally be forgotten in the longer term.

- Simply teaching 'easting first and northing second' accompanied by a good diagram for visual reinforcement has advantages. Using the figures closest to the location in question can be more convenient than referring to the lower and left hand edges of the map. If the map is folded, for example, the figures on its top and right hand edges, or those within the map frame, may be the only ones visible.

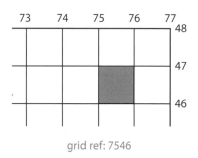

grid ref: 7546

- One option is to use the grid numbers on the bottom and left hand side of the map for initial teaching exercises. The use of grid numbers in other locations could be introduced at a later stage. Many students, however, should be capable of grasping the overall picture from the very beginning if it is well explained and illustrated with good diagrams.

- It is useful to point out that grid reference instructions are usually included in the legend in the event that the system is ever forgotten.

Teaching 6 Figure Grid References

6 figure grid references could be taught indoors as part of an end of day session. If grid squares have previously been used for measuring distance during the day then estimating tenths of a square should be assimilated quite readily. 6-figure references may be better understood if they are illustrated with a good diagram or through using a romer (right).

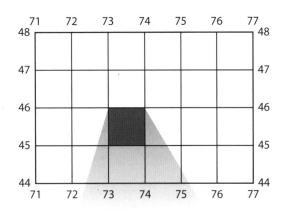

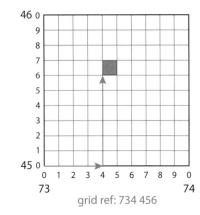

grid ref: 734 456

Grid Reference Letters

Students need to understand that the letters which are included in a full grid reference can, occasionally, be very important.

The National Grid system comprises 625 major squares, each 100km x 100km. Each square is defined by two-letters such as SJ, NR, etc. Many of these squares lie over the sea. The UK mainland, together with its offshore islands, is contained in about 50 of the squares (see diagram, right).

A grid reference with numbers only can apply to any one of these 625 squares! Adding the letters is thus important when communicating with third parties, especially if alerting the emergency services.

The letters for local maps are usually shown on the map legend or in the corner of the map frame. To

confirm the precise location and to reduce the chance of mis-interpretation by a third party, it is important to include a physical description of the location and the name of the nearest village or town.

e.g. SN940646

'Clap Round summit, 4.5km SW of Rhayader in Wales'

If communicating with a non-walker who may be unfamiliar with kilometres, it could be preferable to use miles instead.

				HP	
		HT	HU		
	HW	HX	HY	HZ	
NA	NB	NC	ND		
NF	NG	NH	NJ	NK	
NL	NM	NN	NO		
	NR	NS	NT	NU	
	NW	NX	NY	NZ	OV
		SD	SE	TA	
	SH	SJ	SK	TF	TG
SM	SN	SO	SP	TL	TM
SR	SS	ST	SU	TQ	TR
SV	SW	SX	SY	SZ	TV

Ordnance Survey®

The grid letters of the British mainland

Grid References & Romers

Using a romer to obtain the 3rd and 6th figures of a 6 figure reference is not entirely straight forward. A well-thought tutoring strategy is needed.

There are two requirements for grid references:

• Obtaining the grid reference from a map for a specific feature or position.

• Identifying a feature or position on a map from a given grid reference.

A method for handling the 3rd and 6th figures for both requirements in a simple way that is easy to remember, is shown in the diagram (right).

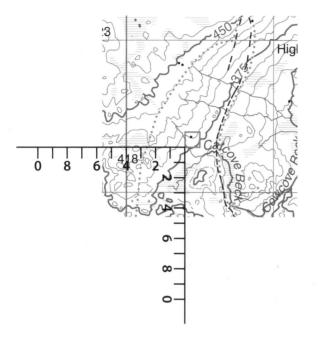

Grid Square

This aid shows a full grid square with all the 100m squares fully visible. It should be easy to see in which square the feature in question belongs and to relate to the corresponding numbers.

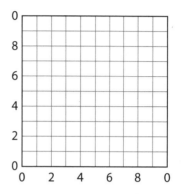

The graduations on the two axes of the romer are aligned exactly against the grid lines leaving no doubt as to which two figures are involved. Students will need guidance on which of the numbers belong to the eastings and northings respectively.

The area relating to these two figures is shown by the red square. The size of the square is one division on the romer scale. The presence of the romer scale provides a physical reference for visualising the size of the square.

Grid Reference Teaching Aids

For students who have problems initially with grid references or romers, the following teaching aids may help.

In each case, graphics software will be needed to produce the diagrams. Several diagrams can be printed on a single transparency which can be cut up to form separate teaching aids.

Whilst aids could be produced for all map scales, too many bits and pieces can be inconvenient to handle. One option is to produce aids for 1:25000 maps only and try to reduce dependency on them after initial exercises. Students will hopefully be able to transfer the skills learned to other map scales.

It is important to use the correct transparency for the specific printer in use. For example, the high operating temperatures of laser printers can melt some transparency materials.

A Romer

This aid is a romer (for use with maps at a scale of 1:25000) with a 100m grid square drawn at its tip for permanent reference. As well as providing an aid for grid reference work, the user can see, very visually, that the small square at the tip is the same size as one division on the romer scale. This should aid the eventual move to using a normal romer.

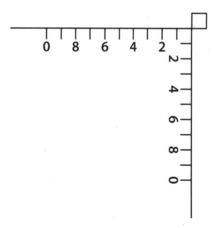

Interpreting Relief

Bronze Navigator students should be able to:

- Recognise whether terrain is uphill, downhill, flat, steep, moderate, etc.

- Recognise prominent hills, valleys, cols, ridges and spurs on a map and be able to identify the corresponding features on the ground.

Smaller contour features are assigned to Silver Navigator and Gold Navigator levels.

Learning Contours Outdoors

In practice most walkers will consider the contour interval only when route planning to calculate times for height gain. Relief interpretation is largely based on experience of comparing map with ground. Very experienced navigators may estimate the physical height of a small feature as an aid to navigation but would rarely attempt to visualise the height of a hill. They may, however, use relative heights as an aid to visualisation e.g. one hill is twice as big as another.

Students can learn contour interpretation outdoors with good tutoring. The key issues are how to go about it and careful choice of tutoring areas.

It is important to emphasize that on any particular map, the vertical contour interval is always constant. It can, however, vary between map types even from the same publisher as shown below.

- HARVEY (1:25000 & 1:40000) - 15m or 10m

- OS (1:50000) - 10m

- OS (1:25000) - 10m or 5m

- Orienteering maps - 5m or 2.5m

Switching between map types may initially create misleading impressions of relief.

Where to Start

The first need is to understand the basic principles of uphill, downhill and steepness. Looking at relief and general landforms should be left until the basic principles have been mastered.

The basic principles are best taught on a suitable walk with the following characteristics:

- Lots of gradient changes in a small area.

- Mainly open terrain to provide a clear view of the gradients.

- Presence of streams.

- Presence of numbered contours.

This route provides various opportunities to compare differing gradients against contour information all within a 3km square

- Streams should be used to confirm uphill or downhill where feasible.

- Numbered contours should be used as an aid to confirm uphill or downhill where feasible.

- Students should realise that a single contour number also indicates the direction of slope. Above the number (in an upright reading position) is uphill and below it is downhill.

- Gradients on the ground should be compared visually with contours and closeness of lines.

- After some practice, try to predict in advance the nature of the next stretch of terrain.

A Walk Along a Contour

A useful reinforcement exercise for contour work is to ask students to imagine that a specific contour line on a map represents an invisible footpath which stays at the same height. Their mission is to try and follow it on the ground. The area used will need to be straight forward and it may be necessary to go off path for short distances.

Following the path of a contour can be a valuable means of practising many aspects of navigation in the attempt to stay on route. Consider the following examples (see diagram on next page):

Contour Walk 1

The route follows the red dot circuit via A-B-C-D.

The first locator will be the wall/fence corner at A.

Following the next section will be reliant on judging distance from the forest boundary to the east.

The first stream provides an opportunity to discuss

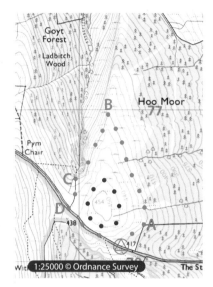

These two exercises involve walking no more than 3km in total and encompass a wide range of navigation skills as well as opportunities to learn lots about contours.

More fun than classroom learning!

how stream flow can be used to verify the direction of slope.

Shortly beyond here the map shows numerical height values. A good place to demonstrate that the orientation of the numbers indicates slope direction.

After the second stream, using the forest boundary as a route locator becomes impractical. Looking along the line of the contour on the map should enable identification of a distant feature to use as a direction fix to proceed to point B.

B provides an ideal opportunity to compare the closely spaced contours to the west against the wider spaced contours to the east and to look at what happens on the ground.

When moving south from B, the obvious valley to the west creates a further discussion point.

From the head of the valley at C, it is necessary to leave the contour line to follow the wall/fence. Here is an opportunity to compare the contours with the gently sloping ground to D.

From D along the road back to the start is initially gently uphill and then downhill.

Contour Walk 2
The blue dotted route follows a short circuit around the summit. Route following relies on estimating a horizontal line, an interesting exercise in itself, and illustrates the difficulty of doing this.

Major Landforms
Students should be able to recognise and use major landforms only, as an aid to accurate route finding. Before embarking on a leg, it is good practice, at any standard of navigation, to use major features to confirm that the route ahead is broadly correct.

Think BIG!

Tutors could encourage students to Think BIG at the start of every leg. Identifying on a map that a route passes to the left or right of a hill, for example, and identifying the corresponding hill on the ground before proceeding, is a key strategy to avoiding major route finding errors. Valleys and cols can be used similarly. In the event of a minor error, at least the navigator will know which valley they are in.

The recognition of landforms can only sensibly be learned outdoors through the continual comparison of an orientated map against ground features. Outdoors is the only place where the true scale and perspective of the terrain is realistic. Considerable support from tutors may be needed initially.

Contour Work Indoors
Looking at contour work indoors during an evening session may be useful to reinforce outdoor learning. Many navigation books have suitable diagrams that might help any students with difficulties.

If forced to work indoors by bad weather, try to have available a means of handling 3-D models e.g. use a small section of map with clear contour features and ask students to create a model of the terrain using playdough, damp sand, etc.

The nearest equivalent to outdoor learning will be via projected slides of terrain which students can compare with a map. However, a photograph will generally distort the perspective of a view. Avoiding extreme wide angle or telephoto zoom settings is the key to the most realistic results. If in doubt, take several shots with different zoom settings and use the best result. A good vantage point is needed to capture relief to best effect.

Orientating a Map against Prominent Contour Features
Whilst listed as a specific skill in the Learning Stages table, students should automatically learn how to do this through the approach advocated for learning contour work outdoors. However they should be aware that orientating the map against prominent ground features is a specific requirement for the Bronze Navigator Award. It is also a key skill when the need for relocation arises.

Using a Compass to Orientate a Map

Compass work at Bronze Navigator level is intended to be kept simple and relevant to the terrain. All compass-related work can be achieved by aligning the compass needle correctly against a north/south grid line and without reference to the dial markings.

In the Bronze Navigator Award, the compass is only used to orientate the map which is itself then used to check the direction of a path in an occasional moment of uncertainty.

Magnetic Variation

At the present time (2010), magnetic variation in the UK is around 2° west and decreasing eastwards by 10' per year. If this trend continues then in 12 years' time magnetic variation will be zero. In 24 years it will be 2° east.

For the next 25 years or so, magnetic variation <u>at this level</u> of navigation can confidently be ignored for practical work! Students should, however be aware of its existence and know that, one day, they may need to take account of it.

Orienteering Maps and Magnetic North

North lines on orienteering maps are always drawn to magnetic north. The map should indicate in which year the north lines were last adjusted. If this is a considerable time ago then use of the map for compass work may be inappropriate.

Orientating a Map with a Compass

The following method provides a simple means of orientating the map without the need for complex compass knowledge.

Before starting, set the North mark on the dial against the Direction of Travel Arrow. This produces a neat and tidy look to reduce complexity and plays no part in the fundamental orientation process.

Other dial markings are not shown on the diagrams as it is unnecessary to use them.

- Put the compass on the map with the needle pivot centred on any N/S gridline. The edges of the baseplate should be parallel with the N/S grid lines and pointing north on the map.

  See diagram 1a

- Hold the compass firmly against the map in front of the body. Rotate body/map/compass as a whole until the north end of the compass needle points northwards along the grid line.

  See diagram 1b

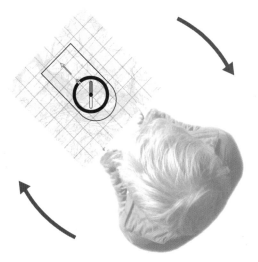

1a - Needle pivot centred on north/south gridline

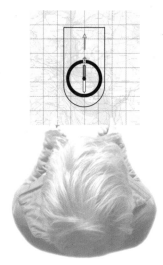

1b - When the map is correctly orientated, everything points north

- The map is now orientated against magnetic north which is sufficiently accurate for bronze navigation decisions.

- With this method, a useful tutoring point is that **when the map is correctly orientated, everything points north** i.e. the map, the body, the baseplate, the dial and the needle.

- Any metal objects in nearby pockets that might affect compass accuracy should be transferred to the rucsac. Close proximity to gates, cars and pylons, etc. should be avoided.

- Mobile phones, whether switched on or off, can also affect compass accuracy significantly. A practical demonstration should prove the most effective means of convincing students to keep them well out of the way.

Checking the Direction of Handrails

With a Compass Orientated Map

- Orientate the map using the previous method.

- The direction of the handrail should now lie in the same direction as the corresponding handrail shown on the orientated map.

- Note that with this method, the direction of a handrail is only checked at a single location.

An Alternative Method

An alternative method that involves sighting with the compass is as follows:

- Align the edge of the compass against the route to be checked (A to B in the example below) and pointing in the same direction as the intended walking route.

- Keeping the compass firmly held against the map in the above position, hold the complete unit in front of the body with the compass pointing outwards from the body.

- Rotate the body/map/compass as a whole until

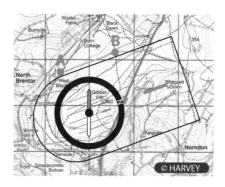

Map orientated to magnetic north with compass base plate and direction of travel arrow pointing in direction of handrail

Checking Direction against Cardinal Points

It is sometimes possible to check a single, isolated handrail against a simple cardinal point. Students should be able to judge N, S, E, W, NE, SE, SW, NW both on a map and against a compass needle.

- Ascertain the cardinal direction from the map.

- Hold the compass in front of the body without the map.

- Judge the cardinal direction of the handrail on the ground against the compass needle.

- Check the cardinal direction from the ground against the one obtained from the map (SE from A to B in the example below).

Baseplate aligned against route to be followed

the compass needle is parallel with a north/south grid line and the north end of the needle points north on the map.

Some students may struggle with holding everything together initially. It is important to keep a check on what is happening.

- The student should now be looking forwards along the direction of travel arrow and along the handrail to be followed. Learning to look along the Direction of Travel Arrow is a useful lead-in to the Silver Navigator Award skills.

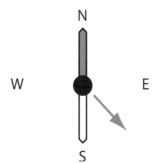

Navigation in Poor Conditions

Navigation in darkness, poor visibility and extreme weather should be discussed as it is unlikely that all these conditions will occur on most courses.

In such conditions, implementation of navigational strategies may be problematic. If displaced for long periods of time, there is potential for psychological problems. Relocation exercises may provide a good opportunity to examine these issues.

Physical Problems
- Difficulty in using the map particularly if refolding is necessary in strong winds.
- Exhaustion from walking in extreme conditions.
- A much reduced field of view in poor visibility.
- A high reduction in visible detail in darkness.

Potential Psychological Problems
- An inclination to lose interest and read the map inadequately through prolonged physical problems.
- Diminished confidence resulting from the inability to see distant landforms when misplaced.

Poor Visibility versus Darkness
It is interesting to compare poor visibility and darkness as they are different in nature.

In really poor visibility in daylight, as caused by cloud and mist, the view ahead will typically be around 20 metres but the detail within that distance will be relatively easy to see. The most unnerving aspect of poor visibility will generally arise from the inability to see major land forms.

In darkness, it is often possible to see well into the distance depending on the degree of cloud cover. With a full moon and no cloud, navigation can almost be as easy as in daylight. Without moonlight,

perspective can change and landform recognition can be problematic. Indistinct paths can sometimes be impossible to see even with a head torch. Paths can disappear in short stretches of tricky terrain such as boulder fields with the exit difficult to find.

Perhaps the most daunting experience may arise from a combination of poor visibility, darkness and rain with the view ahead largely the reflections from a torch beam shining on cloud and raindrops.

Teaching Poor Visibility Navigation
An important aspect of navigation in poor visibility is believing in one's ability to succeed. Attaining such confidence will only come through practice in real, poor visibility conditions. The techniques will largely be those used in normal conditions but with extra care and time taken to remain on course.

Poor visibility may not arise during many courses and night navigation is often used a substitute. As mentioned previously, however, this is not the same as poor visibility in daylight. An alternative, with some similarities, is daylight navigation in woodland

Compass Practice - Woodland can simulate poor visibility

where the view ahead is only 20 metres or so owing to the density of the trees. Such woodland is often found at permanent orienteering courses in areas shown as 'woodland walk' or 'woodland slow run'.

Candidate Experience
Candidates could usefully be advised to experience and practise navigation in poor conditions after obtaining their Award especially if such conditions were not encountered during the course itself. A gradual progression, starting in a relatively secure and well defined area, is the sensible approach.

Even in lowland terrain, high mist density can obscure major features making navigation potentially problematic

Relocation

Relocation can be interpreted in many ways and navigation errors can vary in magnitude depending on the degree of map contact and observation used. It is impractical within the timespan of an NNAS course to cover all eventualities.

It is recommended that tutors cover the basic principles of relocation based on regular map contact and position checks. In such circumstances, a walker should recognise an error within a short space of time and relocate without undue difficulty.

Suggested Approaches for Relocation

The precise approach needed to relocate can only relate to the prevailing circumstances. The ability and confidence to relocate efficiently will improve with experience.

Some useful suggestions are:

- If regular position checks are being made, the walker is unlikely to be more than 1km from their last known position. They should thus be within a circle of 1km radius.

- If the time at which the last location was left is known then the radius of the target circle can be estimated with reasonable accuracy.

- Retrace steps to the last known point?

- Orientate the map with a compass needle.

- If on a track, a distinct line feature or a linear contour feature, check its direction with a compass and look on the map for an equivalent feature running in the same direction.

- If significant landforms are in view, can they be identified on the map?

- Are any streams or rivers visible that compare with map information?

- Are any point features such as farms or churches visible and comparable with map information?

- If none of the above methods help, follow a distinct feature until a positive identification can be made.

Additional suggestions for Silver and Gold:

- In open country, follow a compass bearing to an obvious feature such as a large valley.

- At Gold standard, it may be feasible to judge position by using a transit. Even if the position obtained is approximate, it may be sufficient to use as a basis for subsequently locating a positively identifiable feature by other means.

Tutoring Relocation

The ideal situation for tutoring relocation is when a genuine error has occurred during a training course. However, this may not happen.

Alternatively, take away the maps from the students and ask them to follow the tutor for, say, ten minutes without knowing why. Ideally this will be in a well planned location that offers plenty of features with a variety of position fixing options and solutions.

When the maps are returned, students could be asked to work out where they are as individuals. A subsequent group comparison of decisions and approaches used may prove beneficial. The tutor could provide occasional guidance where necessary.

A summary of relocation techniques may be needed at some stage. A subsequent indoor theory session to back up the outdoor practical work may provide a good opportunity to look at options more generally.

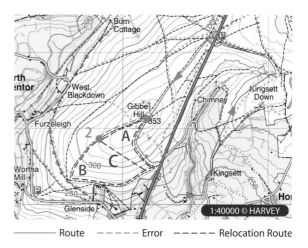

————— Route ————— Error ————— Relocation Route

A simple relocation exercise

The relocation exercise itself need not be complex. It is the principles of the solution that matter most on a training course. The key issues are probably:

- Recognising that an error has occurred.

- Remaining calm and thinking rationally.

In the simple example above, an error occurred at 1 and was recognised at 2. The main options are:

- A - Return to 1 and find the original route.

- B - Descend SW along the path and skirt the bottom of the hill. A slightly longer route.

- C - Descend the hill directly.

Looking at the implications of these options in terms of both good and poor visibility may help to develop rationale in solving problems of this nature.

Sample Routes for the Bronze Navigator Award

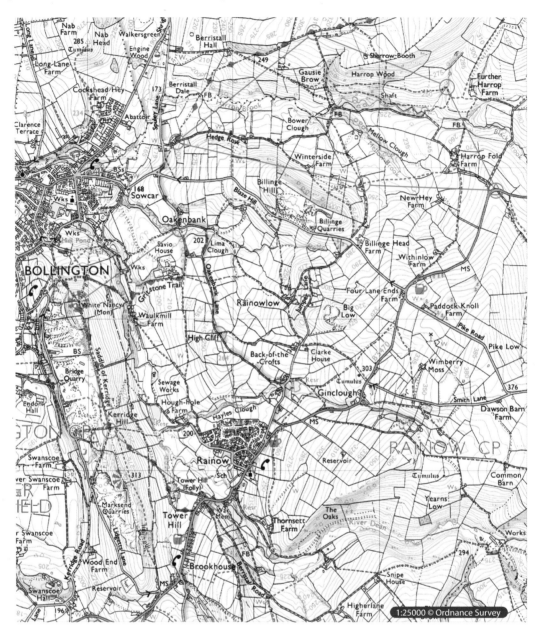

The two circuits, each approximately 5km in length, illustrate good examples of varied terrain with lots of handrails, decision points, route choice and obvious contour features for identifying terrain.

Planning a Bronze Navigator Award Course

It is desirable to plan a course programme which reflects the age, previous experience and specific needs of the students. Where the group is already known to the tutor then planning a good course is relatively straightforward. If the tutor will not meet the group until the first day of the course then a brief chat with the members at the beginning should help establish an appropriate, initial approach to use.

For unknown students, pre-planning a specific tutoring approach can be difficult if not impossible. Having a range of tutoring approaches available to handle differing abilities and levels of knowledge will be especially valuable.

A 'standard' two day programme might typically be used for a group of adults with modest experience of

If a course is being advertised on an open basis then the wording in the advertisement may need some thought, particularly for inexperienced tutors. Stating that a course is aimed at people with no prior walking or navigating experience, for example, should help in assembling a group which is straightforward to teach. Experienced tutors might be able to handle a wide range of abilities without problems.

It may be wise for an advertisement to indicate that receiving the Award is dependent on achieving an appropriate level of performance during the assessment. In some cases, further training may be needed. Under no circumstances should a tutor ever feel obliged to present an award to a person who is not yet competent.

Day 1 Daytime	Work through Stages Table on page 7 to 'Understanding Scales'
Day 1 Evening	Review daytime work Related Topics - Safety, access & Conservation, Weather, etc (some of this should have already been covered during daytime practical work) Walk Planning - To be implemented on Day 2 Preparation for Day 2
Day 2 am	Remaining topics from Stages Table Question & answer session (during lunch?)
Day 2 pm	Assessment Assessment debrief Where next .... Build up experience gradually Consolidate skills before moving on to Silver etc

walking as a member of a led group and who now want to learn to navigate for themselves. Young or inexperienced people may need a course spread over several days with intervals between them.

The table above provides an example of a typical course structure to be used with candidates that have some prior knowledge and experience

Advertising a Course
Often, NNAS courses are run for organisations who have assembled a group of people with similar levels of previous experience. Here, advertising may be unnecessary and devising a suitable delivery strategy should be relatively simple.

Tutoring the Skills of the Silver Navigator Award

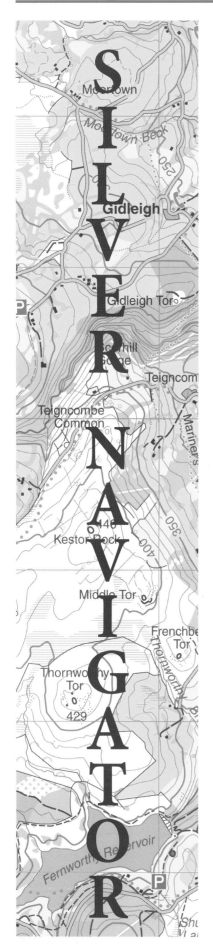

Silver Navigator Award Syllabus

Minimum course duration is 2 days with at least 12 hours of tutor contact time. Additional time may be required for inexperienced candidates.

Maximum tutor/student ratio for training and assessment is 1:6.

The Learning Outcomes

On completion of the Award participants will be able to safely plan and follow a route with some sections away from paths and tracks through being able to:

- Utilise the skills and techniques of the Bronze Award in the context of Silver Award navigation strategies.

- Relate small hills, small valleys, prominent re-entrants and prominent spurs to their corresponding map contours. Use prominent hills, ridges, spurs and valleys as a means of navigation in good visibility.

- Use landforms and point features to orientate the map and as collecting and catching features.

- Use a compass to: accurately follow a bearing; aim off; check the direction of handrails and other linear features.

- Deviate briefly from a compass bearing to avoid obstacles or difficult terrain and accurately regain the original line.

- Use back bearings to check route following accuracy.

- Measure distance on the ground in varied, open terrain using timing and pacing and make practical allowances for any discrepancies.

- Simplify legs using coarse navigation, attack points and fine navigation.

- Recognise dangerous or difficult terrain on a map and on the ground.

- Plan and implement navigational strategies based on the above skills.

- Maintain route finding accuracy in poor visibility or darkness.

- Recognise a navigation error within a few minutes and apply appropriate relocation techniques.

- Understand how personal fitness and nature of terrain affect route choice both at the planning stage and on the ground.

- Understand the potential consequences of fatigue and physical discomfort in demanding terrain and/or extreme weather conditions.

- Select appropriate clothing, equipment and first aid kit for walking in open country in all weather conditions.

- Demonstrate an understanding of the Countryside Code, current access legislation and the environmental impact of walkers on the countryside.

- Understand the responsibilities of walkers towards other countryside interests such as farming, forestry and conservation.

Assessment Guidance Notes

- Practical assessment should take place over a distance of 5km to 8km depending on terrain.

- The assessment route should utilise distinct contour features which require the use of a wide range of navigational strategies.

- The assessment route should offer varied terrain to allow candidates to make appropriate route choice decisions.

- Candidates should plan a safe walk of appropriate distance, explain the issues involved and estimate the time needed for a specific leg.

- Candidates should demonstrate an acceptable level of knowledge of the Countryside Code and Access to Open Country.

Principles for Tutoring the Silver Award

The use of compass techniques and the use of less significant landforms on map and ground represent a significant part of the basis for Silver Navigator Award skills and techniques. Choice of appropriate techniques for specific navigational situations is also a requirement. A reasoned approach to introducing the various techniques is therefore important.

The areas used for learning will ideally have varied hill terrain for contour work along with relatively small stretches of open country for compass work. For contour work, it is often possible to use areas that have been used for Bronze Navigator Award courses but to look at contour interpretation in more detail. Compass work is best practised, primarily, over short distances to maximise the number of exercises and level of reinforcement achieved.

Choice of Areas for Tutoring

Tutoring and practice exercises should take place within the Remit for Course Delivery (p1). The areas chosen should ideally permit plentiful and varied practice of skills.

Tutors could discuss in general terms typical regions, both locally and nationally, for which the Silver Award skills and techniques are most appropriate along with related issues such as:

- Avoidance of straying accidentally into areas which require navigation ability at Gold level.

- Recognising that Silver relocation techniques may be insufficient to be fully confident in complex areas especially in poor visibility.

- Being aware that technical walking skills are just as important as navigation. In particular they should be aware of the potential for straying into terrain which is beyond their walking ability, especially in poor visibility.

Stress that choice of areas for the participants' own ventures is entirely their own responsibility.

Tutoring the Use of Contours

Tutoring the use of contours requires considerable thought and planning. Using contours to maximum advantage is a conceptual process that may prove difficult for some people.

The Extent of Contour Interpretation

Tutors are advised to restrict contour exercises for the Award to those mentioned in the syllabus. Students should be able to navigate using major relief features such as large hills, spurs and valleys. They should also be able to recognise smaller relief features both nearby and in the distance.

There can be no hard and fast rules on the size of smaller features as specific aspects apply such as the distance from the feature. It is suggested that spurs and re-entrants should be around 50m high. Smaller hills should be around 100m higher than surrounding terrain. The diagram below serves as a guide:

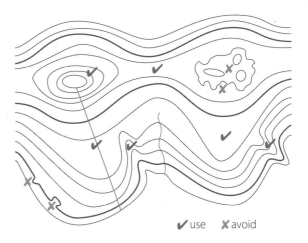

✔ use   ✘ avoid

The red line indicates convex and concave slopes.

The use of small contour features (shown by red crosses) and micro navigation should be left for the Gold Navigator Award.

Constructive Use of Contours

Developing the constructive use of contours can be greatly influenced by the tutoring approach. In particular, the use of well thought out questioning and exercises can help considerably e.g.

- Do you expect the next part of the route to go uphill, downhill or remain level?

- Looking at the map contours, would you expect to be able to see the bottom of the slope when you arrive at its head?

- Would it be quicker to go up and over or around this hill?

- Would it be quicker to cross the valley at this point directly or to walk around its head?

- On a hillside with no paths, use the map and view ahead to choose a sensible ascent route.

- Choose a line of least resistance across this undulating plateau.

Even if a student cannot always answer the question, it will generally serve to provoke interest and imply that the need to learn has some relevance.

Visualisation

The term 'visualisation' is commonly used in relation to viewing the contours on a map and forming a mental image of the terrain ahead to aid navigation. The question arises as to precisely what picture can be expected from a student during a course with a short time span.

The first diagram below shows an orientated map with its contours aligned with the features ahead. Orientating a map requires continual comparison of map and ground until the navigator is satisfied that the map is correctly aligned. Through this process, the skills needed for visualisation should develop.

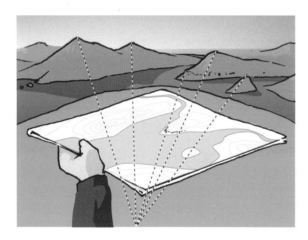

Diagram 1 below shows the view ahead as depicted in the first graphic. The three graphics surrounding it show distorted views which could represent the visualisations obtained by different students. Different interpretations are likely to arise as each individual will have differing abilities to handle the effects of distance, height and perspective. Diagram 2 shows a very simplified interpretation that may be typical of the result attained by many people.

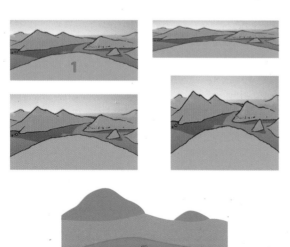

Diagrams courtesy Mountain Training

Introducing Smaller Relief Features

A good introduction to smaller relief features is to view them from close up. A well-chosen route in an area with lots of features will facilitate this exercise. In the example below, following the paths and tracks adjacent to the solid red line would enable many contour features to be examined from close up. Encouraging students to identify as many features as possible themselves is preferable to simply being shown them by the tutor.

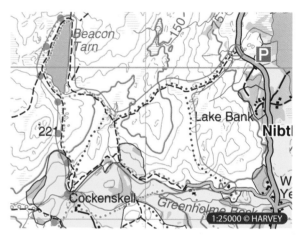

A good route for viewing contour features from close up

The diagram below shows a good example of an area for viewing smaller relief from a distance. No specific route is shown as the whole area is made up of smaller features. Viewing can be from different distances and different directions to add variety to the exercises.

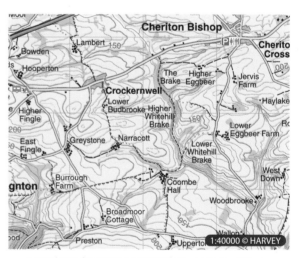

A good area for viewing contour features from a distance

Selecting a Route for Contour Work

The route chosen for contour work can impact on a student's ability to learn effectively. On a linear route, the student will continually move into new terrain throughout the day with continual changes in relief. On a circular route, the same relief will be viewable for longer periods of time and from varying angles, potentially providing a better picture.

Further Contour Exercises

It is useful if a course can include some hill terrain that allows all round practice of Silver Navigator skills and techniques.

In the example below, navigating the route purely by recognising the major ridges, spurs and cols is a key part of the Award. Along the way, any smaller features encountered should also be identifiable.

When viewing from a distance, good features to start with are small cols that are clearly visible on a skyline. The summits on either side of them should be clearly marked with ring contours on the map. If some summits are higher than others, so much the better as it helps in distinguishing one from another. The map below shows some locations with good vantage points for such an exercise.

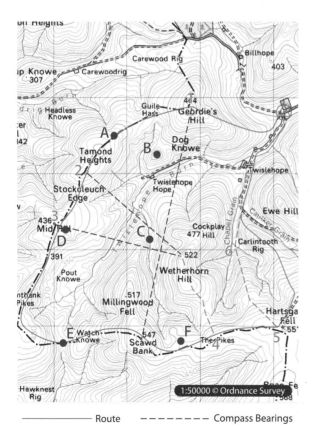

———— Route   — — — — — — Compass Bearings

A good area for all round practice

The route provides opportunities to view summits from different locations in order to see the changing shape as the walk proceeds. Examples of relief and contour exercises in this area are identifying:

- The re-entrant to the northwest of A.
- The knoll B, valley C and col E from A.
- The small spurs at D and F.
- Confirming position at E via adjacent features.

Some students may initially struggle to orientate the map for these exercises. In such cases, setting the map with a compass needle should help to speed up the process. Reducing reliance on the compass should be seen as a priority in terms of developing appropriate skills for the Silver Navigator Award.

Using other learning opportunities can add to the efficiency of the experience. Some possibilities are:

- At 1, 2 & 3, set a compass bearing from the map to the corresponding summit indicated by the dashed purple line i.e. the bearing looking towards the summit.

  Align the compass correctly relative to north and check that the correct summit is in line with the direction of travel arrow.

  Note that back bearings are not included in the syllabus other than as shown on p41.

- At 4, a detour on to Wetherhorn Hill would offer many and varied viewing opportunities. In particular, identifying the summits and cols along the route that has already been walked would be a useful exercise.

- From 4 to 5, half the group uses a pacing measurement and the other half a time. Who achieves the most accurate outcome?

- At 5, descending the alternative route, shown by the dashed red line, enables a comparison of its varying gradients with those seen on the adjacent, more easterly descent.

- At 6, the bottom of the dashed line route, the stream crossing provides an opportunity to look at route choice in relation to avoiding water hazards as the more easterly descent avoids the stream crossing.

These examples illustrate the value of planning good exercises to facilitate learning by experience. The route shown here contains a host of potential learning opportunities besides the ones described.

If looking at topics other than the main theme, try to avoid issues that might cause confusion if covered close together. Looking at relief and water hazards, for example, should be achievable without problem.

Map & Ground Relationships

The way in which people interpret relief is likely to be dependent on experience and the complexity of the terrain. A common approach is to compare map and ground alternately until the walker is confident in how the shape of the terrain matches the map. They may subsequently remember the actual view that they have seen and use that to aid navigation rather than a pure map-based visualisation.

Tutors should accept any workable approach used by students. Full fluency in these skills requires considerable experience that is not likely to be attained within the short timescale of a typical course.

Using Contour Features to Check Position

The presence of general features such as buildings, paths, woodland, ponds, etc for checking route accuracy is not always available in open country. It is sometimes necessary to use relief for this purpose.

In the diagram below, the aim is to locate the small pond at B, starting from position A, using a compass bearing as the prime navigation method. Along the way, are several contour features W, X & Y that could serve as collecting features.

W is the summit of the initial climb and the stream in the dip ahead should be visible. X, at Blawith Knott, is 400m off route and serves as a useful indicator. Y is a small summit close to the route. The 30m height of the feature and its proximity to the streams should serve as a useful discussion point during a training course only. Features of this size are aimed at Gold Navigator level. The prominent summit at Z serves as a catching feature to indicate that an overshoot has occurred if the pond is accidentally bypassed.

The important principle here is that the navigator has recognised the existence of these features before setting out and has a clear strategy in mind for using them to confirm route accuracy.

See p31 for relocation.

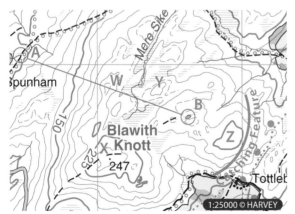

Using collecting and catching features to aid navigation

Coarse & Fine Navigation

Tutors should understand the nature of coarse and fine navigation. The terms originally materialised within orienteering but are applicable to navigation more generally.

Coarse and fine navigation involves 'simplifying' a navigation leg into separate stages that differ in nature. Coarse navigation involves selecting a route that is easy to follow to an 'attack point' using hand-rails and obvious features. The attack point should ideally be a prominent feature that cannot be accidentally mistaken. From the attack point, the navigator proceeds carefully using more intricate techniques to locate the final target.

In the example below, the aim is to locate an aircraft wreck (imaginary) on open moorland. Starting from the road, the route uses coarse navigation to follow obvious tracks and paths to reach a path junction where the route emerges on to the summit area. This junction is the attack point. The fine navigation is a compass bearing down the slope to reach the target.

Using coarse and fine navigation to locate a target

Dangerous Terrain

Using map information, students should know how to recognise or be wary of terrain that could present danger. The most meaningful approach is to visit appropriate locations during a walk to compare map with ground. Students should be encouraged to continue this practice after gaining their award in order to develop the ability to predict from the map, at the planning stage, how feasible a route will be.

The key indicators of dangerous terrain are closely spaced contours, crag or rocky ground symbols and, sometimes, water related symbols. It is important that the student is aware of the representation of such features on different map types. The diagram below shows the differing approaches used on maps at 1:25000 by HARVEY and Ordnance Survey. For other scales, see Maps for NNAS Courses on p13.

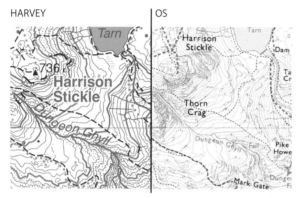

HARVEY   OS

The representation of potentially dangerous ground at 1:25000

If tutors are using orienteering maps for training, danger is recognised via closely spaced contours and cliff/crag symbols. The illustrations below are at a larger scale than is found on maps to make clear the differences. The key identifier for unpassable cliffs is the thicker spine line and shorter tag lines.

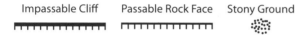

Impassable Cliff   Passable Rock Face   Stony Ground

Orienteering map symbols for potentially dangerous terrain

Unpleasant Terrain

Recognising the potential for unpleasant terrain from map study is not always simple and the walker may need to take into account previous experience of walking in similar areas. Of particular interest are the deep grooves eroded into peat moorland by the action of water and not found in all areas of the country. Avoiding them is a good energy saver.

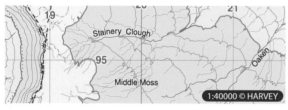

Water erosion in peat moorland can create unpleasant terrain

Water Hazards

Discussing the dangers of water hazards is advised e.g. river crossing (not a practical requirement), flooding and marshy ground. Choosing routes that avoid entrapment by rising water is especially useful.

Tutoring Compass Work

Avoiding Complexity

Compass work can be introduced on a gradual basis, in logical stages, to help students to fully understand the processes involved. It is common practice to teach compass work by rules which may suffice for the duration of the course. However, understanding the processes may remove the need for rules as well as help in remembering the processes themselves.

The impending situation with magnetic variation, in any case, has future implications in respect of using rules to teach compass work.

Magnetic Variation

At the time of writing, magnetic variation is around 2° west of grid north and is decreasing by 10' per annum. If the current rate continues, in 12 years time magnetic variation will be zero and subsequently, east of grid north. Current rules along the lines of 'map to compass - add' will then no longer be valid.

Whilst the relatively low value of magnetic variation for the next few years means that it may be feasible to ignore it in many instances, the tutor should insist on its use for most exercises. The overall aim should be to meet the standard required for the award.

The degree of inaccuracy over a 1km leg for varying values, if magnetic variation is ignored, are shown below. Distances are rounded to the nearest metre.

Variation	Error(1km)
1°	17m
2°	35m
3°	52m

On a practical basis, a figure of 17m per degree per kilometre would suffice. Over longer distances, the higher figures could multiply to become very significant, particularly if route finding in poor visibility.

Ignoring Magnetic Variation

It is important to discuss the implications of ignoring magnetic variation, preferably by using a practical approach e.g. View 2 bearings that differ by 2° over distances of 500m and 1km and view the error against distant features. Repeat with, say, 5°, 10°, etc. Recommendations for long term use might be:

• Setting the map

• Checking the direction of a path or land form

• Bearings over short distances in good visibility

Tutoring Issues

The Problems

Tutors should understand that students may need considerable support when learning compass skills. Some are likely to have problems with accurate implementation of map-based exercises even if they understood the instructions. Further potential for inaccuracies when following a route on the ground is considerable. Novices may often stray 10° or more off course as a result of cumulative errors.

The following issues should serve to highlight the potential for errors during the learning process. It is common for students to understand the process required but struggle to implement them accurately.

- Aligning the compass on the map against start and finish points and not letting it move.
- Reading compass dial graduations correctly.
- Applying a magnetic variation setting.
- Aligning the compass dial base arrows against grid north.
- Aligning the north end of the needle against the base plate reference dots.
- Sighting the line to follow on the ground against the direction of travel arrow.
- Following the route on the ground.
- Continually identifying features to help in maintaining an accurate line.

The Solution?

There is no easy solution. Some people manage to implement compass skills quite accurately without problems. Others may need continual supervision and support over a lengthy period before everything finally clicks.

The most appropriate approach for tutoring is to break down compass skills into gradual and logical stages. This considerably improves the opportunities for students to master any problems one-by-one.

Recognising Compass Work Errors

It is good practice to estimate bearings by simply looking at the map before attempting to obtain a bearing with a compass. Even if the estimate is only to the nearest 10°, it should assist in subsequently recognising a major error, particularly if the error involved is 180°.

Estimating bearings, in any case, helps to reinforce just precisely what they are.

Introducing Compass Work

This section assumes that the tutor is conversant with the various compass techniques and makes no attempt to explain them. It focuses, instead, on learning issues, suggestions for simplifying the learning process and ideas for maximising practise opportunities.

Choosing an Area for Basic Compass Work

A good area for introducing compass work will allow lots of practice of each exercise over short distances. Following a bearing accurately for 2km may be seen as a challenge but ten legs of 200m each enable the student to obtain ten times as much practice at setting the compass. This offers a useful approach for both learning and reinforcing the skills that have been introduced.

Ignoring Magnetic Variation

Ignoring magnetic variation during introductory exercises may help in concentrating on the other issues involved with compass work. Remember, if using a normal walker's map, however, that this will mean continually making allowances for the inevitable errors that will occur.

On an orienteering map, the north lines are aligned to magnetic north. However, they are only accurate at the time the map was produced unless the map has subsequently been realigned against them as part of an update process.

An orienteering map should specifically state the year to which the magnetic north lines apply and it should generally be safe to use the map for up to six years afterwards as the error should be no greater than 1°. If it is significantly beyond six years, then the orienteering map may have little advantage over a walker's map in terms of directional accuracy. If only the map production date is shown, it is wise to be cautious unless the date is recent. If the date of an update is shown, there is no guarantee that the map was realigned against magnetic north at the same time. In the absence of a specific statement about magnetic north, it is best to do a check on the ground to assess the accuracy of the north lines.

The Advantage of an Orienteering Map

An orienteering map at a scale of 1:5000 (or larger) has considerable detail and may offer opportunities for compass legs as short as 100m. This equates to 2cm on the map which is sufficient for aligning the edge of a compass. It may also offer opportunities to look at the principles of various compass techniques such as 'aiming off' or simple back bearings, all within a very confined area.

The following example shows a circuit that would allow lots of practice of various techniques with no leg longer than 150m. The relatively compact area would allow students to function as individuals while the tutor floats between them to check on progress. Working as individuals can help to develop self confidence.

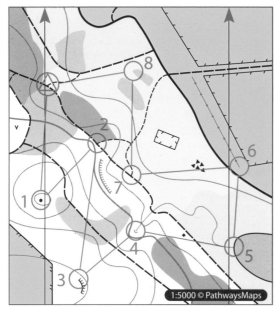

An orienteering map can allow a lot of practice in a small area

A Suggested Tutoring Order

The following list represents a model teaching progression for compass skills. As always, it may need to be adjusted to suit individual circumstances.

Without using Magnetic Variation
In a simple, relatively open area:

- Take a bearing from the map.

- Without moving the dial, hold the compass level in front of the body, pointing straight ahead. Rotate the body and compass as an integral unit until the north end of the needle lies correctly against the reference marks.

- Practise sighting ahead to a distant target with reference to the direction of travel arrow.

- Walk towards the target taking care to avoid straying sideways. Look for intermediate objects en-route to help keep on course.

- In an area of handrails with frequent changes of direction, set the compass bearing of each handrail from the map and use it to check the handrail direction on the ground.

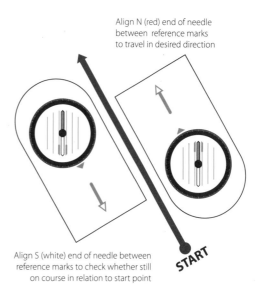

Align N (red) end of needle between reference marks to travel in desired direction

Align S (white) end of needle between reference marks to check whether still on course in relation to start point

START

Pointing a compass back towards the start to check whether still on course. Remember to keep the dial in its original position.

- While moving forward along a handrail, stop and turn to face in the opposite direction so that the south end of the compass needle is aligned against the reference marks. The compass should now point to the start position.

This gives an additional means of checking route-following accuracy without the need for calculations. As the dial has not been turned, the compass is ready for instant use when the desired direction of travel is resumed.

Remember this is a learning exercise. The real value of it will normally be in open country.

- Simple aiming off exercises.

Applying Magnetic Variation
- Introduce magnetic variation preferably by reference to a tutor-drawn magnetic north line on a walker's map. This line should help to show that bearings measured from magnetic north are currently bigger than bearings measured from grid north and that magnetic variation needs to be added.

When students 'add' magnetic variation it is worth checking that the compass dial is turned in the correct direction!

- The progression in the previous section can then be re-applied using magnetic variation.

Magnetic variation is thus being learned against an existing knowledge of compass techniques which should prove less confusing for the student.

Bypassing Obstacles on a Bearing

It is common practice in navigation books to find techniques such as *boxing* recommended to bypass an obstacle and regain the original course. In poor visibility this may well be a potential option.

In good visibility, it will generally be simpler and more efficient to view the ground ahead of the obstacle and look for a feature that is in line with the desired course. It also needs to be feasible to find the feature easily when the obstacle has been bypassed.

The diagram below shows several features that might be visible on the far side of the lake and that are inline or almost inline with the desired course. These are the stream bend, the small crag near the stream bend and the rock cluster just beyond the previous two items. Whilst the end of the crag is not exactly on course, it should be feasible to judge the distance to its left needed to maintain accuracy.

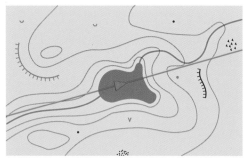

Direction can be maintained by viewing ahead

Distance & Time Estimation

The key requirements for pacing and timing at Silver Navigator Level are:

- Awareness of the issues surrounding accuracy
- More intensive practice than at Bronze level
- Introduction of timing for height climbed
- Use of timing in off-path terrain

Measurement and Accuracy

The fundamental issues surrounding accuracy are covered in *Tutoring the Skills of the Bronze Award*. However, in the Silver Navigator Award, the student will use rougher and more hilly terrain with greater potential for errors. There is also the need to take into account the time required for height climbed which offers further scope for inaccuracies.

Students will need to be more aware of the potential for errors, how to minimise their extent and how to make sensible allowances. Considerable practice will be needed to maximise accuracy.

Timing for Height Climbed & Descended

Measurement of height climbed on the map should be a fairly accurate process as it relies entirely on counting contour lines. However, intermediate undulations on the ground may add to the time needed in practice. What is unpredictable is the rate at which the walker gains height.

Students should understand that calculated times are only an estimate. The actual time taken may be different. On steep ground, for example, the time calculated for height gain alone may be all it takes some walkers to get from bottom to top of a slope.

Whilst it is normal to ignore time for descents, if the descent is on steep or difficult terrain, a time factor may well be involved though hard to calculate.

Vertical Contour Intervals & Timing

A potential problem with calculating the time for height gain is the differing vertical contour intervals used on the various kinds of walking maps.

Rules such as *1 minute per contour* only apply when using Naismith's figures with 10m contours. Some maps, however, have 5m or 15m contours. The method below allows students to ascertain their own height gain rate through experiment.

Tutoring Timing for Height Gained

As with timing for horizontal distance, the time taken to ascend a given height will vary from person to person. Ascertaining a personal figure in the first place seems preferable to using a standard figure that subsequently needs adjusting.

Once again, an individual figure for height gained can be obtained through a simple practical exercise.

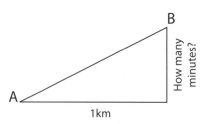

- Find two positions A & B which can be identified on the map as being 1km apart.
- Walk from A to B at a pace that could easily be maintained and note the time taken.
- Each individual can now subtract their figure obtained from walking 1km horizontally. The remainder is the time needed for the ascent.
- A time per 10m (or other convenient height) can now be calculated.

Developing Pacing Skills

Pacing Technique

Measurements should use double paces to reduce the amount of counting required. A greater emphasis should be placed on accuracy for this award as it can be important in open country in poor visibility.

A useful introduction to more accurate pacing is learning to *feel* a stride such that it can be repeated with greater consistency. One approach is to use a relaxed stride and to stop each stride as the leg muscles begin to feel that they would be overstretched were the stride length to be increased further.

An aid to maintaining accuracy is to find 100m stretches with different gradients near home and to check pacing measurements each time they are walked. The footwear worn can affect stride length.

Pacing & Terrain

Pacing on a variety of terrain, uphill, downhill and horizontally, is an important aspect of open country navigation. Developing a good awareness of the extent to which different kinds of terrain can affect pacing accuracy is useful in developing a greater level of accuracy and in making sensible allowances for any discrepancies.

Timing & Position Fixing

Convenient features to confirm position are not always present. Neither can they always be seen in poor visibility. A combination of compass bearings and timing or pacing may provide a solution in some circumstances. Such techniques need to be used with care in areas with steep terrain or crags.

The route to A (left) shows at which points to change direction having followed a specific bearing. The times are based on a walking speed of 3km/h but would need to be adjusted to suit the circumstances.

The object is to keep well away from the streams as, in this area, following them can be unpleasant. Minor errors in timing would simply affect the position at which the edge was finally met. Regaining map contact as soon as possible is good practice.

Using General Relief to Confirm Accuracy

In the absence of point features, using relief to check accuracy may sometimes be the only option.

The route to B (left) follows a direct bearing to aim off to the north of the path bend. The correct route should initially climb gently and then change to traversing the hillside. If straying north, the terrain will remain fairly flat throughout indicating an error. If straying south, the route would run directly downhill with streams ahead as further error indicators.

On the route to A, the steep ground met at the end of the second timed leg serves as a catching feature.

Steep Ground and Contour Lines

The depiction of steep and rocky ground on maps can vary depending on the type of map used. Students should be aware of the differences.

On both HARVEY and OS maps, some contour lines are sometimes omitted on very steep ground as it is impractical to show them all clearly in the available space. Missing contour lines offer a useful indicator of very steep ground.

HARVEY Maps

On HARVEY maps, rocky ground is indicated by grey contour lines. This enables the contours to be seen clearly as they are unobscured by other detail. Some HARVEY maps use coloured height bands where grey shading indicates one of the height ranges. Avoid confusing this with grey contours.

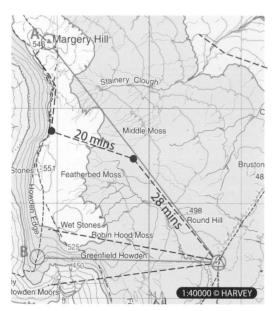

Compass & timing to avoid unpleasant terrain

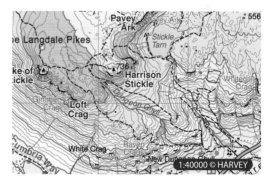

Grey contours on Harvey maps indicate rocky ground

OS Maps

On OS maps, rocky ground is indicated by black squiggles. These stand out clearly but unfortunately tend to obscure the contour detail beneath them. On 1:25000 maps, scree slopes are shown by small black dots as an instant indicator of steep ground. Missing contours also indicate steep ground but more commonly on 1:50000 maps. The effect is rarely present on 1:25000 maps.

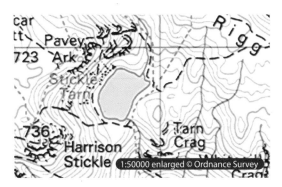

Missing contours indicate steep ground west of Stickle Tarn

Route Planning

As preparation for the route planning element, tutors should use opportunities to discuss planning issues on an ongoing basis during practical work. Comparing a situation on the ground against information on the map is much more meaningful than simply looking at route planning as a theory exercise in a classroom.

Where route choice options exist, consider walking all the options consecutively, even if some are walked in reverse. Students can then learn first hand why one particular option may be better than all the others. In particular, try to find an example where a route that may not be unduly appealing on a fine day may be the best option in poor visibility.

An alternative is to split into small groups with each group walking a different option. At the end of the leg, students can meet up to exchange experiences and try to reach agreement on the best choice.

Sample Routes for the Silver Award

Discussion Points

The route shown on p.45 would be suitable for a training day but would need to be shorter for an assessment. Typical discussion points follow as an aid to developing good route planning strategies.

Start > 1

The northerly route via Shanry has no climbing and a good handrail leads directly to the end of the leg. However, following a stream is not always easy or

safe. With care, it could be used as a reliable route in poor visibility rather than walk the road to the south.

The middle route, involving some ascent, should offer better views and possibly easier walking. It may be more challenging in poor visibility owing to the flat, elongated nature of the summit. A variation is to aim off to the sharp bend in the road near the finish.

1 > 2

The bend in the road offers a clear point from which to aim off to meet the edge of the re-entrant which can then be followed to the top to complete the leg.

2 > 3

This leg could use a direct bearing as the target is fairly large and distinct. The fort to the south would then be used as a collecting feature. Alternatively, the route via the fort might offer greater interest.

3 > 4

The track met on the northerly route serves as a collecting feature. Shortly before the track, the flattening out of the ground serves as an additional collecting feature. This could be very useful in poor visibility to indicate that the track should soon be met especially if the track is not particularly distinct.

The short stretch along the path could be timed to use as an aid in poor visibility as the small hill to the north may not be unduly visible in such conditions.

A direct bearing from the small hill to Arnbathie should suffice in good visibility. Aiming off may be preferable in less ideal conditions.

The southerly route via Goddens offers a more reliable option in poor visibility. The re-entrant, met halfway between Goddens and Arnbathie, serves as a useful collecting feature and lead-in to the target.

4 > 5

The sharp bend in the track provides both a useful collecting feature and an attack point from which to approach Shien Hill. Small hills either side of the route may serve as additional collecting features but may perhaps be a little too small for Silver use. The re-entrant immediately SE of Shien Hill should be identifiable both on route to and from the summit of the hill.

5 > 6

The southerly route via the summit, as ever, is likely to be the more interesting route. However, the summit is relatively flat which may create problems for accurate location in poor visibility. Aiming off to the north of the stream bend may be necessary.

The northerly route avoids climbing by descending

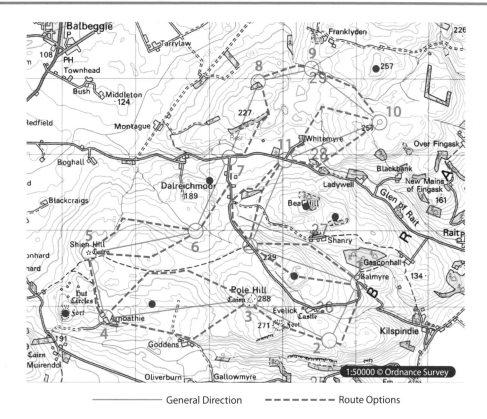

——————— General Direction   ‒ ‒ ‒ ‒ ‒ ‒ ‒ Route Options

This diagram shows typical routes that might be used for Silver Training or Assessment and serves to illustrate principles only. There is no implication that the routes are practical from a legal point of view. The purple spots ● indicate features that a Silver candidate should be able to identify from a distance.

the first stream to the first bend. From here, a more or less horizontal line can be taken to aim off to meet the second stream to the north of the target.

6 > 7

The logical option here is to aim off to meet the road then follow the road to the target. The route offers several contour features and point features to view.

7 > 8

Going east initially to the first road bend provides an attack point for aiming off to the woodland without having to cross the stream. Following the boundary of the woodland to its NE corner provides an attack point for the final target.

Both woodlands will undoubtedly be visible from their respective attack points. This provides a useful indication to the student that the techniques chosen actually work which helps to build confidence.

8 > 9

A straight forward aiming off exercise. The suggested route descends slightly into the valley at a point where it is quite distinct. This may serve as a useful collecting feature in poor visibility.

9 > 10

Following the stream to its source provides an initial attack point for finding the head of the next stream. Between the streams is a small col which should serve as a collecting feature.

10 > 11

The southerly route passes between two areas of woodland which should provide a clear, intermediate target. It does, however, cross a stream.

In wet weather, taking the northerly route via the head of the stream may be preferable.

11 > Finish

The east end of the woods should be clearly visible for normal navigation. Once located, it can be used as an attack point to the target.

In poor visibility, aiming off and following the northern edge of the wood to the road may be simpler, more reliable and quicker.

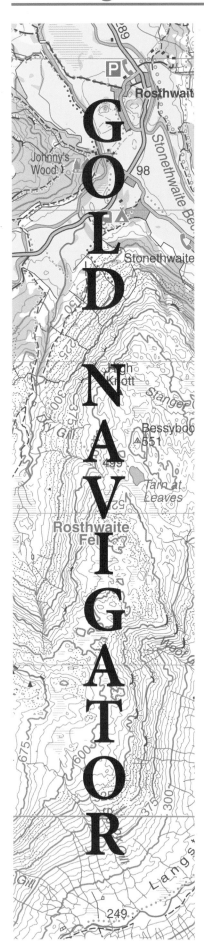

Gold Navigator Award Syllabus

Minimum course duration for training is 2 days with at least 12 hours of tutor contact time. Additional time may be required for inexperienced candidates.

Maximum duration for a separate, practical assessment is 6 hours.

Maximum tutor/student ratio for training and assessment is 1:4.

The Learning Outcomes

On completion of the award, participants will be able to plan and confidently follow safe routes away from paths and tracks in any open countryside through being able to:

- Utilise the skills and techniques of the Bronze and Silver Awards in the context of Gold Award navigation strategies.

- Utilise contours and fine detail as the prime method of navigation.

- Accurately: follow a route, judge distance, check progress against time, use relevant compass skills and maintain continuous map contact.

- Use back bearings and transits to confirm current position.

- Use aspect of slope as an aid to relocation.

- Select appropriate techniques within an overall navigation strategy.

- Navigate in intricate terrain in reduced visibility i.e. mist or darkness.

- Select an appropriate, safe route in relation to height gain and loss, dangerous terrain and other major hazards.

- Assess the route ahead in the field in relation to prevailing conditions or changing circumstances (e.g. weather, time, daylight, ability/fitness) and re-plan the route appropriately if necessary.

- Shorten a route, use an escape route and know emergency procedures.

- Recognise the occurrence of a navigational error within a few minutes and apply appropriate relocation techniques.

- Select appropriate clothing, equipment and first aid for walking in remote areas in all weather conditions.

- Understand the physical demands created by hill and moorland terrain in all weather conditions.

- Understand the effects of cold, heat, fatigue and discomfort on decision making and execution of a selected route.

Assessment Guidance Notes

- Assessment should be taken at a later date in order to provide sufficient opportunity for candidates to practise the required skills.

- Practical assessment should take place over a distance of 6 to 10km depending on terrain.

- The terrain used should include a variety of intricate contour detail along with ridges, valleys and less obvious handrails.

- In the absence of inclement weather or testing conditions, the candidate's awareness and knowledge of navigating safely in such conditions can be ascertained by questioning.

- Candidates should plan a safe walk of appropriate distance, explain the issues involved and estimate the time needed for a specific leg.

- Candidates should demonstrate an acceptable level of knowledge in relevant safety and countryside/environmental issues.

The Gold Navigator Award provides the skills and techniques needed for the the navigator to handle any eventuality. It should be possible to recognise ground features in relation to any information that is shown on the map and use them to follow a safe, logical route through both straightforward and more intricate/complex terrain. In poor visibility, the Gold Navigator should be able to follow a route with considerable ease and confidence.

The Gold Navigator Award is unique within the scheme in that assessment is undertaken at a date subsequent to training to provide candidates with opportunities to hone their skills adequately.

Training Guidance Notes

The choice of areas used for training is critical for maximising learning potential. Whilst this is the scheme's highest award, it does not necessarily translate into high altitude. Remember that many high level walks involve straightforward valleys and ridges with no complexity or intricate navigation.

An ideal area should offer at least the following:

- Opportunities for learning soon after setting out. Terrain for the Gold Navigator Award can be found at relatively low altitudes.

- Terrain with few footpaths or other features that would make navigation too simple for Gold standard.

- Opportunities to apply Bronze and Silver skills in Gold exercises.

- A wide variety of features in a relatively small area for concentrated learning opportunities.

- Opportunities to use both large and small landforms as aiming-off and attack points or as collecting and catching features.

- Terrain which allows route choice and flexible decision making when appropriate e.g. bad weather or fitness/ability strategies and escape routes.

- Avoidance of large areas of tiring ground such as tussocks that would detract from an enjoyable learning experience.

It goes without saying that any area used should be chosen through personal knowledge of the area. It is preferable to check intended routes and learning exercises on the ground in advance to ascertain their practical feasibility and effectiveness. It is especially important to do this to check for risks if intending to send out students on solo exercises.

Maintaining Interest

Students will generally maintain interest better if there is an air of novelty for at least some parts of the course. To that end, it can be helpful to use lively approaches to introduce some teaching exercises.

The section on Occupying the Whole Group (p11) offers several ideas. They encourage concentration on map information, ground features and navigational issues in an enjoyable fashion if presented appropriately. Being unexpectedly asked to follow a route from memory without a map, for example, can evoke a few looks of disbelief initially. However, such exercises soon help to develop confidence as well as creating a pleasant group atmosphere.

Student Centred Learning

During a Gold assessment, the candidate may be given a route with a series of control points. They will be asked to identify the most appropriate route between successive controls and to follow it using relevant skills and strategies. They may also be asked to explain their choices. To that end, students should learn Gold standard navigation through being asked to make decisions from the very beginning to encourage and develop navigational reasoning.

After making a choice, they can discuss decisions with the tutor who can give appropriate feedback along with alternative approaches. The student is thus given a degree of responsibility but learns from the tutor alongside it. Another advantage is that the tutor is seen to be displaying an interest in student progress. An alternative approach is to use peer group discussions on route choice and navigation strategies with occasional tutor intervention where clarification of any uncertainties is needed.

In the earlier stages, tasks could relate to applying Bronze or Silver techniques to Gold navigation tasks. Tasks can become progressively more demanding as the student develops increasing knowledge and understanding.

The key to success with this approach is for tutors to use both probing and open-ended questions. A question that can simply be answered *yes* or *no* gives no feedback on the student's thought processes.

"What made you choose this route rather than that route" or "Why might this route be easier to follow than that one" require explanation and reasoning from the student. Such responses not only provide information about the student's understanding but also make it easier for the tutor to feed back relevant advice on subsequent processes.

Choice of Maps

Standard walking maps at scales of 1:25000 and 1:40000 will generally be appropriate. Orienteering maps of a sufficiently large area at a scale of 1:15000 may also be suitable if they allow training and assessment in the full range of skills and knowledge. However, be aware of the following issues if using orienteering maps for assessment purposes:

- Suitable orienteering maps will generally have been produced for competition purposes and not all clubs will provide or allow use of them for casual or recreational purposes.

- Unavailability of an orienteering map during the consolidation period means that the student may have little, if any, regular experience of using them.

  It should be feasible to interpret relief and make route choice decisions but in the absence of adequate practice opportunities, distance judgement may not be fluent.

Tutors may need to make allowances for such issues.

Choosing Suitable Routes

When planning potential routes for both training and assessment, the following criteria should be considered:

- The routes should include varied contour information that might be encountered in the course of a normal walk.

  This would include some major features as well as simple but less distinct features such as small ridges, spurs, re-entrants, etc.

  Fine contour interpretation should form only part of the techniques used.

- Routes should allow practice or assessment of many skills in a small area.

Route Choice Exercises
- Route choice over long distances may be best implemented as a theory exercise in order to allow maximum time for other issues.

- Practical route finding exercises may be better suited to shorter distances.

- Students could be asked to plan a route between two controls and then explain their reasoning for the choice.

- Route choice exercises can alternatively be based on specific criteria as choices are often related to other factors e.g.

  The fastest route

  The best route in a NW gale force wind

The best route in heavy rainfall

The route that minimises ascent and descent

- Choosing different criteria for each student allows different routes to be used between controls for solo navigation. It also allows the tutor to judge the student's ability to plan with reference to specific circumstances.

Routes Across the Ground
An often forgotten aspect of navigation is the line taken across the ground as opposed to general directional accuracy. Walking in a straight line may require the negotiation of tiring terrain. Looking ahead may reveal a winding route offering optimum conditions underfoot and low energy consumption though the target needs to be kept firmly in view.

A useful exercise is to indicate a distant feature and ask candidates to follow the most efficient route to it using nothing more than observation.

An opposite exercise is attempting to maintain a straight line without the continual use of a compass. This would entail continually looking ahead for features that are in line with the current one.

Compass Exercises

The use of a compass in Gold courses should be seen as an aid to navigation by relief, when needed, rather than a substitute for it. Students should additionally demonstrate an ability to navigate purely against major relief and small contour detail.

The following techniques are necessary:

- Following a bearing with a good degree of accuracy over short and long distances. A long distance could be regarded as 1 - 2km in terms of course time limitations.

- Accurate bypassing of obstacles on the route.

- Using relief to confirm position when following a bearing.

- Using a transit to confirm position along a distinct linear feature.

- Using a transit as an aid to relocation.

  In the absence of a distinct linear feature, a transit can sometimes allow an approximate fix that can be fine-tuned by other methods.

- Estimating position using aspect of slope.

Initial Exercises

Using a carefully chosen area with short distances, minimal climbing and plentiful features allows intensive, varied and valuable learning experiences. The example below is contained within a 2km square and is adjacent to a road which avoids a long walk-in.

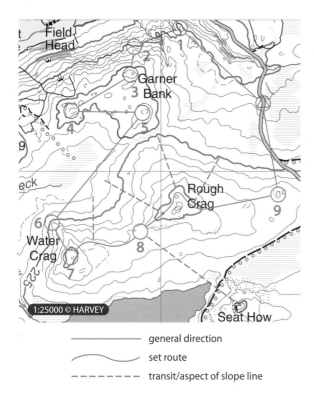

Start > 1

This could be followed with a compass bearing with the student asked to identify the shapes in the index contour as they are met.

1 > 2

Continuing to follow the path of index contour allows further identification of various features until the small spur is met below Garner Bank. Grey contours are present to identify rocky ground.

2 > 3

Continuing up the spur leads to further grey contours with a ring contour indicating a rocky summit.

3 > 4 > 5

A tour of the summit plateau with several small contour features to identify.

5 > 6

This route crosses a grey contour spur. Prior recognition could lead to slight southerly detour to follow the re-entrant WSW then alongside the marshy area.

6 > 7

Follows a well-defined small spur to the summit. The presence of grey contours should again result in some debate about route choice.

7 > 8 > 9

The defined route along the northern edge of the ridge provides opportunites to look at aspect of slope. At 9, a back bearing can be taken from either Seat How or the eastern end of the lake to use as a transit to locate the current position along the ridge.

Contour Only Exercises

Using a contour only map is an excellent means of focusing a student's attention on how contours can be used. Even in a relatively simple area, a contour only exercise requires a great deal of concentration.

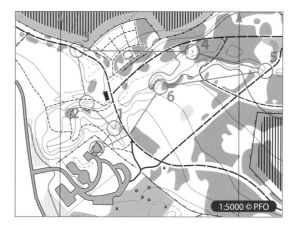

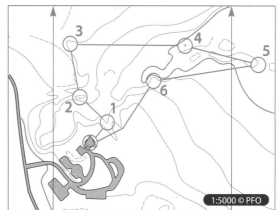

The example above shows a short circuit in a town park. Following the route using the contour map means that obstructions will be encountered. Accurate circumvention of them means maintaining close contact with the contour information.

HARVEY will produce contour only extracts of its maps. Orienteering clubs should be able to provide them for their maps as the mapping software enables unwanted map symbols to be easily hidden.

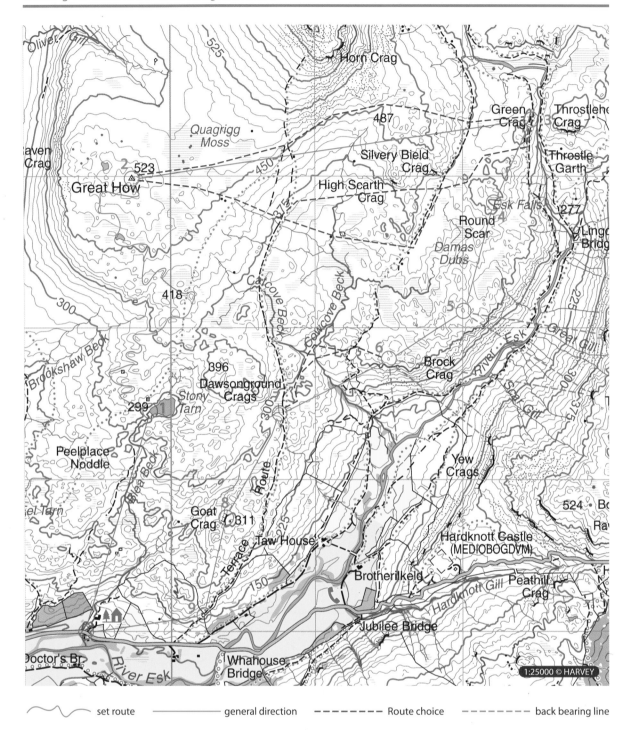

~~~~ set route ———— general direction ------- Route choice ------- back bearing line

A Variety of Exercises

The route above offers an interesting learning experience through varied exercises/approaches.

Start > 1

Students will be asked to follow the stream on the ground and use the contour only map (next page) to plot its approximate line. Use of the normal map is not allowed. This is a fun way to focus on contour information using an unexpected approach. It also brings in many other aspects of navigation.

1 > 2

Students follow the route of the curvy line marked on the normal map, as precisely as possible. A great way to focus on specific contour detail, map orientation and constant map contact.

2 > 3

A major route choice exercise to facilitate discussion of the issues involved. The options shown provide opportunities to look at avoidance of water hazards or minimising the problems of them.

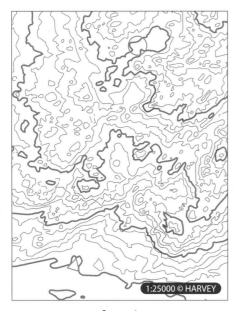

Start > 1
Plot the line of the stream followed on the ground

3 > 4 > 5

These legs provide an opportunity to navigate from memory. The student studies the map, memorises the relevant information then tries to navigate to the next control without a map (taken away by tutor). The two legs offer differing kinds of contour information to add variety. Memory exercises encourage the student to focus on the most useful and minimal information needed for route following.

5 > 6

An opportunity to look at back bearings and using transits to fix position on a line feature. In this case the line feature is the top of the steep, SE facing slope. The same leg could be used to practise aspect of slope.

6 > 7

A second opportunity to look at route choice and water hazards. The northerly detour avoids losing height. The more northerly of the two detour options crosses the stream above the confluence which is sometimes a safer choice.

7 > 8

The obvious route choice here is via the index contour detail immediately west of the general direction line. This leads on to the small stream which provides an attack point for the next control.

8 > 9

A straightforward leg with various route options available for discussion.

Gold - Specific Assessment Issues

Direct Entry

Direct entry into Gold assessment is not advisable. Candidates are recommended to attend at least a refresher course or a Silver assessment beforehand.

Timing & Pacing

Timing and pacing measurements should generally be achieved with a high degree of accuracy though allowances may be necessary in some circumstances e.g.

- Terrain which is unusually difficult underfoot and the candidate could not reasonably be expected to have previous experience.

- Terrain which could not reasonably be predicted from map information.

- Extreme weather conditions.

Candidates should nevertheless be able to make efficient allowances for related errors. Assessors should ideally avoid such problems by using areas that allow reasonable estimates to be made.

Techniques to Avoid in Assessment

Whilst the use of resections and boxing may be mentioned briefly during a training course, they are not considered essential skills but can be items in a tool box. Transits are generally adequate for position fixing. Avoiding obstacles when using a compass bearing in good visibility can generally be achieved by simpler and more efficient methods.

Maps for Assessment

It is preferable to use areas where assessments can use normal walking maps for at least some of the route. Where contour detail is badly obscured by rock symbols, it may be feasible to use a 1:50000 scale map enlarged to 1:25000 or an orienteering map for some of the time. If there is a HARVEY map of the area, the rock symbol issue is avoided.

Remember that candidates may not have access to enlarged maps for their own walks. Use of enlarged maps or orienteering maps for a whole assessment is therefore questionable as a means of assessing navigational ability.

Candidates should use different maps during the various stages of the course but all candidates should use similar maps for any given exercise. The use of different types may inadvertently place one candidate at an advantage or disadvantage to the others.

Assessing the NNAS Awards

Assessment is the process through which a candidate's performance is judged against a set of criteria to justify eligibility for an Award. Anyone who assumes the role of an assessor automatically adopts a high level of responsibility both to the candidate and to the reputation of the scheme.

In the event that a pass is given to a candidate who has not achieved the requisite level of performance, the credibility of the scheme is at stake. An assessor equally needs to perform impeccably to avoid the situation whereby a candidate fails to achieve competence through the assessor's own shortcomings.

It follows that any assessment requires careful thought, planning and implementation in order to facilitate a 'fair playing field' for the candidate. The overall aim must be to create a situation that allows the candidate to demonstrate their true ability. Any assessment should be fair and consistent with avoidance of subjectivity on the part of the assessor.

Assessment Protocol

Fair assessments have become a key issue nowadays with all awarding organisations. Most use a similar basic model commonly known as the 7 Steps.

the **7** *steps*

1 Preparation

- The venue should be well suited to the skills and techniques for the particular award level.

- Avoid areas which have serious map errors.

- Potential routes and tasks need to be planned in advance to ensure that the candidate has ample access to opportunites to demonstrate their competence through practical exercises.

- Plan in advance supplementary exercises such as questioning and identifying distant landforms along with when they will be used to minimise interference with the main tasks.

- Ensure that each candidate is given tasks that are broadly similar in nature and standard.

- All exercises should be straightforward and unambiguous navigation tasks.

- How the group will be organised e.g. whole group together, sent out individually, etc.

2 Briefing

- The candidate should receive a clear briefing that indicates how the assessment will be run.

- The standard required for the award should be outlined.

- What happens if a candidate strays off route or recognises an error?

- If the whole group is together with one person navigating, how will the remainder be assessed?

- How candidate competence will be assessed and the assessor's general approach.

- An opportunity for candidates to clarify any aspect of the assessment before starting.

3 Observation & Analysis

- Once an assessment task has commenced, the assessor should not intervene other than in exceptional circumstances such as unsafe practice or unrecognised major errors.

- If a navigation error occurs, the candidate should be allowed to proceed without any indication of concern from the assessor. Recognising an error and correcting it is a valid part of an assessment.

- For how long an error is allowed to go unrecognised is at the assessor's discretion depending on the circumstances.

- In the event of inadequate performance, it will be necessary to record what went wrong for subsequent feedback. Accurate analysis and identification of the problem is essential.

- Recording positive aspects of performance is equally valid to justify a pass. It is also useful to indicate specific strengths to the candidate.

- Recording will inevitably be in the form of note taking. However, this should be achieved discretely to avoid unnerving the candidate.

4 Questioning

- The only need for questioning is for extracting additional knowledge from the candidate prior to making the assessment decision. This may be on completion of a practical exercise, typically at the end of a leg. It may also occur as the final part of the assessment process if the assessor wishes to clarify any overall aspects of the candidate's performance.

- Questioning is not a part of the debrief process.

- Questions need to be relevant to the Award level and asked in a manner that keeps the candidate relaxed. Showing an interest in the candidate's responses is good practice.

- Questions ideally need to be asked such that answers require reasoning or multi-word responses.

e.g. A candidate who has identified a distant land-form in relation to the map can be asked to suggest two supporting pieces of evidence.

- Questions along the lines of, "How do you think you did?" are not really relevant to a pure skills assessment. They are normally used in coach assessments to indicate that a coach is capable of analysing their own performance. If absolutely necessary, it is preferable to ask, "Is there anything that you think you did particularly well?"

- Be prepared to re-phrase a question if the candidate does not understand the original.

5 Decision & Feedback

- The decision is given first as a straight statement of *competent* or *not yet competent*.

  The decision should be based only on quantifiable evidence from the assessment process.

- The feedback should indicate the reasons for the assessment decision.

  Feedback should be based on observations and recorded evidence from the assessment process.

6 Action Planning

- Regardless of whether a candidate is competent or not yet competent, they should leave an assessment with a clear picture of their abilities, strengths and weaknesses, etc.

- An action plan should not only provide advice on how to polish up on any minor aspects of the assessment but should also suggest ways of moving forward with navigational ability.

7 Documentation

- The assessor should process efficiently any paperwork connected with certificate claims so that candidates receive their awards with the minimum of delay.

- Keeping written evidence of assessment performance for all candidates is important. A not competent candidate may subsequently appeal or the competence of a successful candidate may be challenged by a third party. The need for evidence in such cases is obvious.

Other Assessment Issues

Maps for NNAS Assessment

It will generally be necessary to use a standard scale walking map to facilitate assessment of all the skills. Orienteering maps do not generally offer sufficient scope to test all skills and should be used with care. Remember that NNAS Awards are meant to indicate competence at using walking maps.

Assessment Ratios

The recommended maximum staff/candidate ratios for assessment are:

- Bronze & Silver - 1:6

- Gold - 1:4

Handling even these numbers can be challenging and inexperienced assessors may well benefit from seeking additional assistance.

Keeping the Whole Group Occupied

The aim of an assessment is to gather evidence to support a competence decision. Keeping all candidates active for most of the time maximises the opportunities for gathering such evidence. The ideas suggested in the tutoring section for occupying a whole group are generally valid for assessments.

Assessment Management

There are several ways of handling the group though it is important to consider the overall objectives of the assessment when deciding which format to use.

An NNAS Award holder should be competent to plan and implement a day walk independently. Keeping a group together for the whole assessment offers no opportunity to judge a candidate's confidence to navigate without moral support. It is thus preferable to include an element of solo navigation.

Some possibilities for this are:

- Set up several (one per candidate) short loop courses that return to a central control point. Each loop could require different skills. Candidates can be sent individually around different loops before returning for another one. The assessor could discuss the strategies used on completion of each loop.

- Set up several linear routes that all pass through two or three check points with helpers used to monitor them.

- The assessor sends each candidate ahead to locate different features or locations. These can be either along the route or slightly off it. They wait at the position concerned until the assessor comes along shortly afterwards to check that they are in the correct place.

- Ask candidates to individually walk the path of a contour line which passes through or close to obvious features. This shows that candidates have interpreted the map information correctly.

- Without using a map, walk a short leg with several features then ask candidates to draw a simple map of the route taken. Alternatively, the map could be constructed with natural materials such as twigs or blades of grass. This tests the candidate's ability to assimilate useful and relevant information.

- In a relatively small area, set up in advance a number (e.g. 10) of check points each with a control marker and ID code. Allocate to each candidate a unique route e.g.

  Candidate 1 - 1, 2, 4, 6,10

  Candidate 2 - 2, 3, 5, 8, 7

  Candidate 3 - 3, 6, 7, 8, 9

  Candidates note down the ID markings as proof that they have visited the check points.

Remember that group exercises may only imply that each candidate has passed through the check points. There may be no evidence of who did the navigating unless the assessor can supervise the area from a high vantage point. Good questioning techniques may be of value in such circumstances.

If a candidate does not succeed at a solo task and the assessor has not witnessed the performance directly then providing accurate feedback at the end will be difficult. Use of solo exercises as the only means of assessment is therefore not advisable.

If a candidate becomes lost during a solo leg, the assessor could potentially have to abandon the assessment to conduct a search. A clear briefing on the prodedures to use in such circumstances may help. For example is there an obvious feature visible from a distance that could serve as muster point? Having an assistant to conduct a search could be useful.

Related Topics & Theory Papers

Bronze and Silver courses are generally run on two consecutive days with little opportunity to assimilate information. It is therefore suggested that assessment should mostly relate to navigation only. A Silver candidate should, however, demonstrate an outline knowledge of access issues and sources of weather forecasts.

An indoor route planning exercise for the Bronze or Silver awards is acceptable. Other aspects of navigation theory should preferably be tested orally in the field through reference to real terrain and features.

For the Gold award, a higher level of knowledge is essential particularly in respect of access and safety. There is time between training and assessment to assimilate such information. A theory paper may maximise the time available for practical work. One option is a home paper completed in advance with oral questioning on the answers to ascertain that they are the candidate's own work. A very short paper (20 minutes?) on the day, covering a few key

issues, could be used to supplement this.

Gathering Evidence

Evidence of competence should be obtained through setting a task and observing the approach used. The candidate may use a different strategy to that expected by the assessor but if it works then it should generally be accepted. If it is necessary to see a technique which has not been demonstrated then a specific exercise could be set at a later stage.

The Assessment Decision

In considering competence, it will be necessary to review only the objective evidence obtained against the award criteria. Subjectivity should be avoided.

The assessor must decide whether the candidate is *Competent* or *Not Competent*. If found to be not competent, the normal outcome will be an action plan followed by a full re-assessment at a later date.

It will be necessary to consider the following:

- Was the candidate able to choose and implement appropriate techniques/strategies?
- Were good routes chosen across the ground?
- To what extent did the candidate make errors?
- One or two small errors quickly recognised and corrected is a competent decision.
- Continual errors or not recognising a major error would be a not competent decision.
- Was the route completed within or reasonably close to the candidate's estimated time?
- Was the performance fluent and confident?

Assessment Appeals

A candidate who is dissatisfied with an assessment decision may appeal against it. Details of the process can be downloaded from the NNAS website.

Tutor Development

It is good practice for tutors to develop their own delivery methods for the benefit of their students. The approach needed will vary according to the tutor's existing experience.

Personal Research

There are plenty of magazine articles and literature available on aspects of practical navigation but little written on how to teach it. With a little imagination, experienced tutors can use such sources to make some progress with new ideas.

NNAS Workshops

The National Navigation Award Scheme offers workshops that are normally focussed on specific aspects of tutoring. These are advertised on the NNAS website and provide an ideal opportunity for development. Inexperienced tutors can learn from other delegates and experienced tutors can exchange views and ideas.

Working Alongside Other Tutors

Looking at how other people deliver courses can sometimes be of value. Seeing just a single good idea in practice can influence the future approach used in a wider sense. The NNAS website has a list of registered providers, and tutors could contact some of them to discuss the possibility of meeting up.

1st4sport Certificate in Tutoring Sport

Experienced navigators with no background in tutoring may well benefit from formal training.

1st4sport is a specialist sports awarding body that offers a variety of coaching qualifications. The Certificate in Tutoring Sport is a generic award that covers tutoring principles rather than specific sports.

The training course (over two days) covers:

- Planning training to suit student learning styles
- Planning and delivering interactive learning sessions
- Questioning and feedback techniques

There is a subsequent consolidation period in which to practise the subject matter. Assessment is via a home paper and a one hour practical session tutoring a real group.

Information can be obtained from 1st4sport at www.1st4sportqualifications.com

Certificates in Coaching Orienteering

UKCC Certificates in Coaching Orienteering are awarded at levels 1, 2 & 3 by 1st4sport Qualifications in partnership with British Orienteering. A slant towards performance makes the awards more appropriate for tutors at Silver and Gold Navigator levels. Prior research on usefulness is recommended.

British Orienteering Teacher Courses

British Orienteering offers two Teaching Orienteering Courses (Parts 1 & 2). Each course is a separate attendance-only day for teachers, youth workers and similar personnel. They are offered through British Orienteering and cover the basics of tutoring the skills and techniques of orienteering. Inexperienced NNAS tutors may find these courses of some value. There is no formal assessment and the cost of the courses is usually very reasonable.

The combined courses provide ideas for tutoring methods up to NNAS Silver Navigator standard. For tutors who work with young people, the courses also introduce several ideas that add interest and fun to learning. NNAS tutors may need to adapt some of the methods advocated to make them more suited to tutoring walking navigation.

Part 1

Part 1 covers use of school grounds or similar for learning basic techniques such as:

- Understanding the map
- Orientating the map
- Following simple line features
- Relating map to ground

Part 2

Part 2 covers use of small local parks to introduce topics such as:

- Basic compass work (magnetic north only)
- Aiming off
- Use of attack points
- Distance estimation by pacing
- Footpath symbols
- Collecting and catching features
- Vegetation symbols
- Identification of simple relief features

Information can be obtained from British Orienteering at www.britishorienteering.org.uk.

Sources of Relevant Information

Access

England: Natural England
www.naturalengland.org.uk
The booklet **Countryside Code** provides the basics.
Downloadable booklet (ref: NE326).
Information on rights of way and access land; links to the Countryside Access site which gives more information.

Wales: Countryside Council for Wales
www.ccw.gov.uk

Scotland
www.outdooraccess-scotland.com
Provides official information on access.

Ramblers
www.ramblers.org.uk
Has detailed information (including arrangements in Scotland) with links to further information.

Conservation

British Mountaineering Council
www.thebmc.co.uk
The 'access & conservation' page offers the downloadable BMC **Green Guide to the Uplands**.

Mountain Training
www.mountain-training.org
The book **Hillwalking** (ISBN 0954151100) includes a section on the upland environment.

Scottish Mountaineering Club
www.smc.org.uk
The book **Hostile Habitats** (ISBN 0907521932) is totally devoted to conservation.

Scottish Natural Heritage
www.outdooraccess-scotland.com
'Access Code Advice for Recreation Users' > 'Responsibilities' is a download on responsibilities.

Mountaineering Council of Scotland
www.mcofs.org.uk
'Access and Conservation' > 'Conservation' has useful information on conservation.

Scottish Environment Link
www.scotlink.org
Links to Scottish environmental organisations.

National Parks
www.lakedistrict.gov.uk
www.peakdistrict.gov.uk
www.eryri-npa.gov.uk
Discussion and examples on footpath erosion.

Emergencies

Hillwalking (ISBN 0954151100) & BMC booklet **Safety on Mountains** are starting points for examining the causes.
www.mountain.rescue.org.uk > Mountain Advice

For basic emergency planning and procedures
Web search 'rescue & emergency care' or 'ITC' for providers.

Maps

HARVEY
www.harveymaps.co.uk

Ordnance Survey
www.ordnancesurvey.co.uk

Digital Mapping
www.anquet.co.uk   www.routebuddy.com
www.avenza.com/pdf-maps   www.viewranger.com
www.memory-map.co.uk

Navigation Hardware

Compasses
www.suunto.com
www.silvacompass.com

GPS
www.satmap.com
www.garmin.com

Books

Hillwalking, *Mountain Training*
ISBN 0954151100
Provides good coverage of hillwalking in general.

Navigation in the Mountains, *Mountain Training*
ISBN 9780954151157
Definitive guide for hill walkers, mountaineers & leaders. The official navigation book for all ML Training Schemes.

Map & Compass, The Art of Navigation, *Pete Hawkins*
ISBN 9781852843946
Good coverage of navigation skills and techniques.

Navigation for Walkers, *Julian Tippett*
ISBN 1871890543
A different approach using map illustrations and related photographs of the terrain.

Teaching Orienteering, *McNeil, Cory-Wright, Renfrew*
ISBN 0880118040 published by HARVEY
An in depth study of coaching orienteering with many ideas that are adaptable for tutoring walking navigation.

Cicerone Press
www.cicerone.co.uk
A good selection of books on walking & mountaineering.

Organisations

National Navigation Award Scheme
www.nnas.org.uk
Tutor support materials + Information on the scheme.

British Orienteering
www.britishorienteering.org.uk
Information on orienteering, orienteering clubs and teaching orienteering courses.

1st4sport Qualifications
www.1st4sportqualifications.com
Level 3 Certificate in Tutoring in Sport
UKCC Level 1, 2 & 3 Certificates in Coaching Orienteering.